DIGITAL MARKETING MASTERY

Strategies and Techniques for Business Growth

By
Danish Ali Bajwa & Usama Bajwa

Copyright © 2023 By RK Books Publication

The content contained within this book may not be reproduced, duplicated, or transmitted in any form or retrieval system now known or to be invented without direct written permission from the author or publisher. Under no circumstances will any blame or legal responsibility be held against the publisher, or author, for any damages, reparation, or monetary loss due to the information contained within this book. Either directly or indirectly.

Legal Notice:

This book is copyright protected. This book is only for personal use. You cannot amend, distribute, sell, use, quote, or paraphrase any part of the content within this book without the author or publisher's consent. "Fair Use" means a summary or quote with appropriate credit to the author is permitted.

Disclaimer Notice:

Please note the information contained within this book is for educational purposes only. All effort has been executed to present accurate, up-to-date, reliable, and complete information. No warranties of any kind are declared or implied. Readers acknowledge that the author is not rendering legal, financial, medical, or professional advice. The content within this book has been derived from various sources. Please consult a qualified professional before attempting any techniques outlined in this book. By reading and using this book, the reader agrees that under no circumstances is the author responsible for any direct or indirect losses incurred due to the use of the information within this book, including, but not limited to, — errors, omissions, or inaccuracies.

Email: rkbooks16@gmail.com

EBOOK ISBN: 978-969-3492-03-3

PAPERBACK ISBN: 978-969-3492-04-0

HARDBACK ISBN: 978-969-3492-05-7

Authors Bio

Danish Ali Bajwa and Usama Bajwa, collectively known as the Bajwa Brothers, are a dynamic writing duo known for their vast array of published works spanning several genres. Born and raised in a home where creativity and knowledge were deeply valued, these brothers harnessed their intrinsic knack for storytelling and exploration into a thriving career in literature.

Danish Ali Bajwa is a prolific writer with a unique ability to connect with a diverse audience. With a distinct voice, he has contributed to an extensive collection of children's books, where he elegantly interweaves essential life lessons with engaging narratives that resonate with young minds. Beyond children's literature, Usama's portfolio also includes a number of motivational books. He has an uncanny knack for uplifting and inspiring readers through his compelling narratives and authentic portrayals of the human spirit. Usama's words serve as a beacon of positivity, inspiring readers to conquer their fears and reach their true potential.

Usama Bajwa, on the other hand, brings an analytical perspective to their writing collaboration. With a keen interest in the intersection of business and technology, Danish has written several informative books, making complex topics accessible and engaging for readers. Danish's expertise in business and tech-related subjects is evident in his comprehensive and intuitive guides. He excels at presenting innovative ideas and futuristic trends with a grounded understanding of contemporary business needs, making his books a staple in the libraries of ambitious entrepreneurs and tech enthusiasts.

Together, Danish and Usama have cultivated a unique and diverse writing style that captivates their readers, keeping them engrossed from the first page to the last. Their books often reflect the symbiosis of their different interests and expertise, and the powerful balance between emotion and logic. Despite their varied interests, they share a commitment to creating high-quality literature that is both engaging and enlightening. The Bajwa Brothers continue to establish their presence in the literary world, building a legacy of insightful, thought-provoking, and enchanting books that truly make a difference.

Table of Contents

Introduction 1

Chapter 1 Introduction to Digital Marketing 4

    Understanding the Digital Marketing Landscape 4

    Evolution of Digital Marketing 6

    Importance of Digital Marketing for Business Growth 8

Chapter 2 Defining Your Digital Marketing Goals 11

    Setting SMART Goals for Digital Marketing 11

    Aligning Business Objectives with Digital Marketing Goals 13

    Establishing Key Performance Indicators (KPIs) 14

Chapter 3 Building an Effective Digital Marketing Strategy 18

    Conducting Market Research and Competitor Analysis 20

    Identifying Target Audience: Creating Buyer Personas 21

    Identifying Target Audience and Creating Buyer Personas 23

    Conducting Surveys and Interviews 24

    Choosing the Right Digital Marketing Channels 26

    Understanding Different Digital Marketing Channels 26

Chapter 4 Website Optimization and User Experience 29

    Designing a User-Friendly Website 32

    Consistent Branding and Visual Design 33

    Implementing Search Engine Optimization (SEO) Techniques 35

    Enhancing Website Performance and Mobile Optimization 38

Chapter 5 Content Marketing and Storytelling 42

    Crafting Compelling and Relevant Content 45

    Implementing Content Distribution Strategies 48

Chapter 6 Social Media Marketing 52
    Developing a Social Media Strategy 54
    Engaging with Followers and Building Brand Loyalty 58
    Leveraging Social Media Advertising 60

Chapter 7 Search Engine Marketing (SEM) and Pay-Per-Click (PPC) 64
    Understanding Search Engine Marketing (SEM) and its Benefits ... 67
    Creating Effective PPC Campaigns 69
    Optimizing Ad Performance and Measuring ROI 72

Chapter 8 Email Marketing and Automation 76
    Designing Impactful Email Campaigns 79
    Implementing Marketing Automation Tools 81
    Personalization and Segmentation 86
    Creating Dynamic Content 91

Chapter 9 Influencer Marketing and Brand Partnerships 93
    Identifying the Right Influencers 94
    Consider influencer partnerships and collaborations 98
    Measuring the effectiveness of influencer campaigns 101

Chapter 10 Analytics and Performance Tracking 104
    Setting up analytics tools (Google Analytics, etc.) 107
    Analyzing key metrics and interpreting data 110
    Making data-driven decisions for continuous improvement 112

Chapter 11 Emerging Trends and Future of Digital Marketing 116
    Exploring the latest trends and technologies 119
    Preparing for future shifts in the digital marketing landscape 122
    Harnessing the power of artificial intelligence and automation ... 124

Chapter 12 Creating an Actionable Digital Marketing Plan 128

Pulling all the elements together into a cohesive plan 131
Budgeting and resource allocation 133
Monitoring, testing, and optimizing strategies 136
Conclusion **142**

Introduction

"Digital Marketing Mastery: Strategies and Techniques for Business Growth" is an in-depth and comprehensive guide that aims to empower business owners, entrepreneurs, and marketing professionals with the knowledge and skills needed to excel in the ever-evolving world of digital marketing. As technology continues to reshape the way we connect, communicate, and consume information, it has become crucial for businesses to establish a strong online presence and effectively engage with their target audiences.

In this digital age, traditional marketing strategies alone are no longer sufficient to drive sustainable growth. Digital marketing offers a vast array of opportunities and channels to reach and connect with customers, enabling businesses to expand their reach, enhance brand visibility, and drive measurable results. However, navigating the complex and ever-changing digital landscape can be overwhelming, especially for those new to the field or struggling to keep up with the latest trends and techniques.

This book serves as your comprehensive roadmap to mastering digital marketing. It is designed to provide a solid foundation of knowledge and equip you with practical strategies and techniques that have been proven to generate results. Whether you are a small business owner looking to establish an online presence, an entrepreneur aiming to launch a successful digital startup, or a marketing professional seeking to upgrade your skills, this book will serve as your trusted companion.

Throughout the pages of this book, we will explore a wide range of topics, starting with an introduction to digital marketing and its evolution. We will delve into the fundamental concepts and principles that underpin effective digital marketing strategies, ensuring you have a strong understanding of the core elements needed for success.

We will guide you through the process of defining clear and achievable digital marketing goals, aligning them with your overall business objectives, and establishing key performance indicators (KPIs) to track and measure progress. You will learn how to conduct market research and competitor analysis, identify your target audience, and create detailed buyer personas to guide your marketing efforts.

Building upon this foundation, we will delve into the essential components of a robust digital marketing strategy. We will explore website optimization techniques to improve search engine rankings, enhance user experience, and maximize conversions. Content marketing will be examined in detail, providing insights into crafting compelling and engaging content across various formats and channels.

Social media marketing, search engine marketing (SEM), and pay-per-click (PPC) advertising will also be explored, offering guidance on leveraging these powerful tools to expand your reach, drive targeted traffic, and increase conversions. Email marketing strategies, including automation and personalization, will be covered to help you nurture leads, build customer loyalty, and achieve higher conversion rates.

In addition, we will delve into influencer marketing and brand partnerships, exploring how to identify relevant influencers, establish fruitful collaborations, and measure the effectiveness of such campaigns. Analytics and performance tracking will also be discussed in detail, enabling you to make data-driven decisions, optimize your marketing efforts, and achieve continuous improvement.

Moreover, we will examine emerging trends and future directions in digital marketing, equipping you with insights into the latest technologies and innovations shaping the industry. We will explore the role of artificial intelligence and automation, and how you can leverage these advancements to gain a competitive edge.

To help you apply the knowledge gained throughout this book, we will guide you in creating an actionable digital marketing plan. We will discuss budgeting and resource allocation, and emphasize the importance of monitoring, testing, and optimizing your strategies to ensure ongoing success.

By the end of this book, you will have a comprehensive understanding of digital marketing and the strategies and techniques needed to drive business growth. You will be equipped with practical knowledge, real-world examples, and valuable insights to navigate the dynamic digital landscape with confidence. Whether you are a digital marketing novice or an experienced professional, "Digital Marketing Mastery: Strategies and Techniques for Business Growth" will be your go-to resource for mastering the art and science of digital marketing.

Chapter 1
Introduction to Digital Marketing

Understanding the Digital Marketing Landscape

In today's interconnected world, digital marketing has become an indispensable tool for businesses seeking to thrive in the competitive marketplace. In this chapter, we delve into the intricate and dynamic landscape of digital marketing, exploring its various components and how they intersect to create a holistic marketing ecosystem.

We begin by defining digital marketing and its significance in the modern business environment. Digital marketing encompasses a broad range of online marketing activities that leverage digital channels, such as websites, search engines, social media platforms, email, and mobile applications, to connect with target audiences and drive desired outcomes.

Next, we explore the digital marketing channels available to businesses, understanding their unique characteristics, advantages, and considerations. We delve into search engine marketing (SEM) and search engine optimization (SEO), which focus on improving visibility and driving organic and paid traffic from search engines. We also examine social media marketing, content marketing, email marketing, display advertising, and other prominent channels that enable businesses to engage with their audiences in meaningful ways.

Additionally, we discuss the importance of mobile marketing, considering the exponential growth of mobile device usage and its impact on consumer behavior. Mobile optimization, responsive design, and the rise of mobile applications are all crucial aspects of a comprehensive digital marketing strategy.

Furthermore, we explore the concept of user experience (UX) and its role in digital marketing. Understanding how to design intuitive and user-friendly interfaces, optimize website performance, and create seamless customer journeys are key considerations for successful digital marketing campaigns.

As we progress, we delve into the significance of data-driven marketing and the utilization of analytics tools. We discuss the importance of tracking and measuring key performance indicators (KPIs), such as website traffic, conversion rates, customer engagement, and return on investment (ROI). By harnessing the power of data, businesses can gain valuable insights into customer behavior, preferences, and trends, enabling them to make informed marketing decisions.

Moreover, we explore the interplay between digital marketing and traditional marketing methods. While traditional marketing remains relevant, digital marketing offers unique advantages, including real-time feedback, precise targeting, and the ability to customize and personalize messaging. We discuss the integration of digital and traditional marketing strategies to create cohesive and impactful campaigns.

By the end of this chapter, readers will have a comprehensive understanding of the digital marketing landscape, including its various channels, considerations, and the importance of data-driven decision-making. This knowledge will serve as a solid foundation for the subsequent chapters, where we delve deeper into specific digital marketing strategies and techniques for business growth.

Evolution of Digital Marketing

In this chapter, we embark on a journey through the evolution of digital marketing, tracing its roots from the early days of the internet to its present-day prominence in the marketing landscape. Understanding the evolution of digital marketing allows us to appreciate its transformative power and the significant impact it has had on businesses worldwide.

We begin by exploring the birth of the internet and its profound influence on communication and information sharing. With the advent of the World Wide Web, businesses gained a new platform to showcase their products and services to a global audience. Early websites served as digital brochures, providing basic information and contact details.

As the internet continued to evolve, so did digital marketing. The emergence of search engines, such as Yahoo, AltaVista, and eventually Google, sparked the need for businesses to optimize their online presence. Search engine optimization (SEO) became a critical aspect of digital marketing, allowing websites to rank higher in search results and attract organic traffic.

The introduction of social media platforms, including MySpace, Facebook, Twitter, and Instagram, revolutionized how people connected and interacted online. Businesses quickly recognized the potential for social media marketing, leveraging these platforms to engage with customers, build brand communities, and foster brand loyalty.

The rise of mobile devices further accelerated the evolution of digital marketing. With smartphones becoming an integral part of everyday life, businesses had to adapt their strategies to cater to a mobile audience. Mobile-responsive websites, mobile apps, and location-based marketing strategies emerged to meet the growing demands of consumers on the go.

The era of big data brought a new dimension to digital marketing. With the ability to capture and analyze vast amounts of customer data, businesses gained valuable insights into consumer behavior, preferences, and purchase patterns. This data-driven approach empowered marketers to personalize their messaging, deliver targeted advertisements, and optimize campaigns for maximum impact.

Technological advancements, such as artificial intelligence (AI), machine learning, and automation, have further transformed digital marketing. AI-powered chatbots streamline customer interactions, while automated email marketing workflows nurture leads and drive conversions. Programmatic advertising algorithms optimize ad placements, targeting the right audience at the right time with precision.

Today, digital marketing continues to evolve at a rapid pace. The introduction of voice search, virtual reality (VR), augmented reality (AR), and other emerging technologies present new opportunities and challenges for marketers. Staying abreast of these developments is crucial for businesses aiming to stay competitive and effectively engage their target audiences.

By understanding the evolution of digital marketing, we gain insight into its historical context, milestones, and the underlying factors that have shaped its current landscape. This knowledge provides a foundation for exploring the strategies and techniques covered in subsequent chapters, allowing businesses to leverage the full potential of digital marketing to drive growth and success.

Importance of Digital Marketing for Business Growth

In this chapter, we delve into the fundamental reasons why digital marketing is crucial for businesses seeking sustainable growth and success in today's highly competitive marketplace. As technology continues to advance and consumer behavior evolves, businesses must adapt their marketing strategies to leverage the power of digital channels.

First and foremost, digital marketing offers unparalleled reach and accessibility. The internet has connected people from around the world, providing businesses with a global platform to showcase their products or services. With a well-crafted digital marketing strategy, businesses can transcend geographical boundaries and target specific audiences with precision. This level of reach and accessibility opens up new growth opportunities and enables businesses to expand their customer base exponentially.

Digital marketing also provides targeted audience engagement. Unlike traditional marketing methods, digital marketing allows businesses to identify and engage with their ideal customers more effectively. Through various digital channels, businesses can gather data on consumer preferences, behaviors, and demographics. This data can then be used to create personalized and relevant marketing messages, increasing the chances of capturing the attention and interest of potential customers. The ability to deliver targeted messages to the right audience at the right time significantly enhances the efficiency and effectiveness of marketing efforts.

Furthermore, digital marketing offers measurable results and a higher return on investment (ROI). Unlike traditional marketing channels, which often rely on estimates and assumptions, digital marketing allows for precise tracking and measurement of key performance indicators (KPIs). Businesses can monitor metrics such as website traffic, conversion rates, engagement levels, and sales data in real-time. This data-driven approach enables businesses to optimize their campaigns, identify areas for improvement, and allocate resources more efficiently. The ability to measure and analyze marketing efforts ensures that businesses can make data-backed decisions, resulting in a higher ROI and a more effective use of marketing budgets.

Digital marketing also fosters customer engagement and relationship building. Through social media platforms, blogs, email marketing, and other digital channels, businesses can engage in two-way communication with their customers. This enables businesses to listen to customer feedback, address concerns, and build a sense of trust and loyalty. By providing valuable and engaging content, businesses can establish themselves as thought leaders and build lasting relationships with their customers. The ability to cultivate meaningful connections with customers contributes to long-term business growth and customer retention.

Finally, digital marketing offers flexibility and agility. In the fast-paced digital landscape, businesses need to be adaptable and responsive to market trends and consumer demands. Digital marketing allows for quick adjustments and modifications to campaigns, ensuring that businesses can stay relevant and maintain a competitive edge. The ability to test, iterate, and optimize marketing strategies in real-time provides businesses with the agility needed to seize emerging opportunities and respond to changing market dynamics.

In conclusion, digital marketing is of paramount importance for business growth in today's digital age. Its wide reach, targeted engagement, measurability, customer relationship building, and flexibility make it an indispensable tool for businesses aiming to thrive and succeed. By embracing digital marketing strategies, businesses can unlock new growth opportunities, reach their target audiences effectively, and achieve sustainable business growth.

Chapter 2
Defining Your Digital Marketing Goals

Setting SMART Goals for Digital Marketing

In this chapter, we delve into the process of setting clear and actionable goals for your digital marketing endeavors. Without well-defined goals, businesses may struggle to measure progress, allocate resources effectively, and ultimately achieve meaningful results. By following the SMART framework, businesses can ensure their digital marketing goals are Specific, Measurable, Attainable, Relevant, and Time-bound.

We begin by emphasizing the importance of specificity when setting digital marketing goals. Vague or broad goals can lead to confusion and lack of direction. Instead, goals should be specific and well-defined, outlining the desired outcome in detail. For example, a specific goal could be to increase website traffic by 20% within the next six months.

Next, we explore the concept of measurability in goal setting. Effective digital marketing goals should be quantifiable, allowing businesses to track progress and determine success. Measurable goals enable businesses to collect and analyze data, providing insights into the effectiveness of their marketing efforts. Examples of measurable goals include increasing social media engagement by 25% or achieving a 15% conversion rate on a specific landing page.

Moreover, we discuss the importance of setting attainable goals that are realistic and feasible given the resources and capabilities of the business. While it is essential to aim high, setting unattainable goals can lead to frustration and demotivation. By setting goals that challenge but are within reach, businesses can maintain momentum and a sense of accomplishment as they make progress.

Relevance is another critical factor in goal setting. Digital marketing goals should align with the overall business objectives and contribute to the growth and success of the organization. Each goal should have a clear connection to the broader marketing strategy and support the business's long-term vision. Ensuring goal relevance helps maintain focus and ensure that efforts are directed toward meaningful outcomes.

Lastly, we emphasize the importance of time-bound goals. Without a specific timeframe, goals may lack a sense of urgency and may not drive action. Setting a deadline creates a sense of accountability and provides a framework for planning and execution. Businesses should establish realistic timelines for achieving their digital marketing goals, considering factors such as seasonality, market conditions, and available resources.

Throughout this chapter, we provide practical examples and guidance on how to apply the SMART framework to digital marketing goal setting. We discuss common pitfalls to avoid and provide tips for overcoming challenges that may arise during the goal-setting process. By the end of this chapter, readers will have the tools and knowledge to define clear, actionable, and SMART goals that will guide their digital marketing strategies and contribute to the growth and success of their businesses.

Aligning Business Objectives with Digital Marketing Goals

In this chapter, we delve into the crucial process of aligning business objectives with digital marketing goals. A strong alignment between the two ensures that digital marketing efforts are purposeful, focused, and contribute directly to the overall success of the business.

Understanding Business Objectives

To begin, we emphasize the significance of clearly defining and understanding the business objectives. These objectives serve as the foundation for the entire organization and guide decision-making at all levels. Business objectives may include increasing market share, expanding into new markets, boosting sales revenue, improving customer retention, or launching new products or services. By understanding the broader objectives, businesses can identify how digital marketing can support and drive these goals.

Identifying Digital Marketing Opportunities

Once the business objectives are clear, the next step is to identify the digital marketing opportunities that align with those objectives. This involves conducting a thorough analysis of the target market, customer preferences, competitive landscape, and available resources. By understanding the market dynamics and customer behavior, businesses can pinpoint the specific digital marketing channels, strategies, and tactics that will be most effective in achieving the desired business outcomes.

Defining Digital Marketing Goals

Based on the identified opportunities, businesses can then define their digital marketing goals. These goals should be aligned with the broader business objectives and contribute directly to their realization. For instance, if the business objective is to increase market share, a corresponding digital marketing goal could be to expand brand awareness and reach a larger audience through targeted social media campaigns or search engine optimization efforts. By aligning the digital marketing goals with the business objectives, businesses ensure that their efforts are focused and have a direct impact on overall growth.

Establishing Key Performance Indicators (KPIs)

To track progress and measure the success of digital marketing initiatives, businesses need to establish key performance indicators (KPIs). KPIs are specific metrics that reflect the achievement of digital marketing goals. They can include metrics such as website traffic, conversion rates, customer engagement, return on investment (ROI), or social media followers. By setting clear KPIs, businesses can monitor and evaluate the effectiveness of their digital marketing strategies and make data-driven decisions to optimize their efforts.

Continuous Evaluation and Adaptation

Lastly, we highlight the importance of continuous evaluation and adaptation in the alignment process. Business objectives and market dynamics can change over time, and digital marketing strategies need to evolve accordingly. Regularly reassessing and realigning digital marketing goals with business objectives ensures that the strategies remain relevant and effective in driving growth. By staying agile and responsive to market changes, businesses can optimize their digital marketing efforts and seize emerging opportunities.

Throughout this chapter, we provide practical insights and examples to illustrate how businesses can align their digital marketing goals with their broader business objectives. By aligning these two critical components, businesses can maximize the impact of their digital marketing strategies and achieve meaningful and measurable results that directly contribute to overall business growth and success.

Establishing Key Performance Indicators (KPIs)

In this chapter, we delve into the process of establishing Key Performance Indicators (KPIs) for digital marketing. KPIs play a vital role in tracking progress, evaluating success, and optimizing digital marketing efforts. By defining clear and relevant KPIs, businesses can effectively measure their performance and make data-driven decisions to drive growth and achieve their digital marketing goals.

Understanding Key Performance Indicators (KPIs)

To begin, we provide an in-depth understanding of what KPIs are and their significance in digital marketing. KPIs are specific metrics that reflect the performance and progress towards achieving digital marketing goals. They provide a quantifiable way to measure success, evaluate effectiveness, and identify areas for improvement. KPIs can vary depending on the nature of the business, the specific digital marketing objectives, and the channels or tactics employed.

Aligning KPIs with Digital Marketing Goals

The next step is to align the chosen KPIs with the digital marketing goals established earlier. KPIs should directly reflect the desired outcomes and provide insights into the effectiveness of the strategies and tactics employed. For example, if the digital marketing goal is to increase website traffic, relevant KPIs could include metrics such as the number of unique visitors, page views, or the bounce rate. By aligning KPIs with goals, businesses ensure that they are tracking the right metrics that directly contribute to their desired outcomes.

Choosing Relevant and Measurable KPIs

When selecting KPIs, it is essential to choose those that are both relevant and measurable. Relevant KPIs are directly related to the specific goals and objectives of the digital marketing campaign. They provide meaningful insights into the progress towards those goals. Measurable KPIs, on the other hand, are quantifiable and allow for tracking and comparison over time. This ensures that progress can be objectively assessed and measured. By choosing relevant and measurable KPIs, businesses can gain a clear understanding of their performance and make informed decisions.

Utilizing a Balanced Set of KPIs

A balanced set of KPIs provides a comprehensive view of the performance across different aspects of digital marketing. It includes a combination of leading indicators, such as website traffic or social media engagement, as well as lagging indicators, such as conversion rates or customer lifetime value. This balanced approach enables businesses to monitor both short-term progress and long-term success. By utilizing a range of KPIs, businesses gain a holistic understanding of their digital marketing performance.

Monitoring, Analyzing, and Optimizing

KPIs Once the KPIs are established, it is crucial to regularly monitor, analyze, and optimize based on the insights gained. Businesses should utilize analytics tools and reporting mechanisms to track the selected KPIs. Regular monitoring allows for timely identification of trends, patterns, and areas for improvement.

Analyzing KPI data provides valuable insights into the effectiveness of digital marketing strategies, highlighting what is working well and areas that require adjustment. Optimization involves making data-driven decisions and implementing changes to enhance performance and maximize results.

Throughout this chapter, we provide practical guidance on establishing relevant and measurable KPIs for digital marketing campaigns. We emphasize the importance of aligning KPIs with goals, choosing a balanced set of metrics, and continually monitoring and optimizing performance. By effectively utilizing KPIs, businesses can track progress, measure success, and make informed decisions to drive growth and achieve their digital marketing objectives.

Chapter 3
Building an Effective Digital Marketing Strategy

In this chapter, we delve into the process of building an effective digital marketing strategy. A well-crafted strategy serves as a roadmap for businesses, outlining the steps and tactics required to achieve their digital marketing goals and drive sustainable growth. By following a systematic approach, businesses can maximize their digital marketing efforts and effectively engage their target audience.

To begin, we discuss the importance of conducting thorough market research and competitor analysis. Understanding the market landscape and competitive environment is crucial for identifying opportunities, differentiating the business from competitors, and tailoring marketing messages to resonate with the target audience. Market research provides insights into customer preferences, behaviors, and trends, while competitor analysis helps businesses identify their strengths, weaknesses, and unique selling propositions.

Next, we delve into the process of identifying and understanding the target audience. By creating detailed buyer personas, businesses gain a deep understanding of their ideal customers, including demographics, interests, pain points, and motivations. This information enables businesses to tailor their digital marketing strategies to effectively reach and engage with their target audience, ultimately driving higher conversion rates and customer loyalty.

Choosing the right digital marketing channels is another crucial aspect of building an effective strategy. We discuss the various channels available, including search engine marketing (SEM), social media marketing, email marketing, content marketing, and more. Each channel has its strengths and characteristics, and businesses should select the ones that align with their target audience preferences and business objectives. Understanding the unique advantages and best practices of each channel empowers businesses to allocate resources effectively and optimize their digital marketing efforts.

Furthermore, we explore the significance of content marketing in driving digital marketing success. Content is the backbone of digital marketing, enabling businesses to engage, educate, and inspire their audience. We discuss the importance of creating high-quality and relevant content across various formats, such as blog articles, videos, infographics, and podcasts. Developing a content distribution strategy ensures that the right content is delivered through the appropriate channels, maximizing its reach and impact.

In addition, we emphasize the role of social media marketing in building brand awareness, fostering customer relationships, and driving conversions. We discuss strategies for creating engaging social media content, leveraging user-generated content, and utilizing social media advertising to target specific audience segments effectively. Understanding the dynamics and best practices of social media platforms enables businesses to leverage their power in reaching and engaging with their audience.

Measurement and analytics play a critical role in optimizing digital marketing strategies. We discuss the importance of implementing analytics tools, such as Google Analytics, to track and measure key performance indicators (KPIs). By analyzing data and monitoring the performance of various digital marketing initiatives, businesses can gain valuable insights, identify areas for improvement, and make data-driven decisions to optimize their strategies continually.

Finally, we emphasize the importance of continuous learning and adaptation in the ever-evolving digital marketing landscape. Digital marketing strategies need to be flexible and adaptable to stay ahead of the curve. Monitoring industry trends, staying informed about emerging technologies, and testing and iterating strategies are vital for maintaining a competitive edge and driving continuous improvement.

By the end of this chapter, readers will have a comprehensive understanding of the key components involved in building an effective digital marketing strategy. They will be equipped with the knowledge and tools to conduct market research, define target audiences, select appropriate channels, create compelling content, measure performance, and adapt their strategies for long-term success in the dynamic digital marketing landscape.

Conducting Market Research and Competitor Analysis

In this chapter, we explore the crucial steps of conducting market research and competitor analysis as part of building an effective digital marketing strategy. These activities provide valuable insights into the market landscape, consumer behavior, and competitor positioning. By understanding the market dynamics and competitive environment, businesses can identify opportunities, differentiate themselves, and tailor their digital marketing strategies to resonate with their target audience effectively.

Market Research: Understanding the Landscape

We begin by emphasizing the importance of conducting comprehensive market research. Market research involves gathering and analyzing data related to the target market, industry trends, customer preferences, and market demand. It helps businesses gain a deep understanding of the market landscape, enabling them to make informed decisions and develop strategies that align with market needs. Market research methods can include surveys, interviews, focus groups, and analyzing industry reports and data.

Identifying Target Audience: Creating Buyer Personas

Next, we delve into the process of identifying and understanding the target audience. By creating detailed buyer personas, businesses can develop a clear picture of their ideal customers. Buyer personas are fictional representations of the target audience, including demographic information, interests, pain points, motivations, and behavior patterns. This understanding enables businesses to tailor their digital marketing strategies to effectively reach and engage with their target audience, delivering the right messages through the right channels.

Competitor Analysis: Understanding the Competitive Landscape

Competitor analysis is another crucial component of market research. It involves evaluating the strengths and weaknesses of competitors, their market positioning, and their digital marketing strategies. By studying competitors' websites, social media presence, content, advertising campaigns, and customer reviews, businesses can gain insights into what is working well and identify areas of opportunity. Competitor analysis helps businesses differentiate themselves, understand industry benchmarks, and identify strategies that can give them a competitive advantage.

Identifying Opportunities: SWOT Analysis

As part of market research and competitor analysis, conducting a SWOT analysis is highly beneficial. SWOT stands for Strengths, Weaknesses, Opportunities, and Threats. It helps businesses identify their own strengths and weaknesses, as well as opportunities and threats present in the market and competitive landscape. By understanding these factors, businesses can capitalize on their strengths, address weaknesses, exploit opportunities, and mitigate potential threats. The SWOT analysis serves as a foundation for developing a targeted and effective digital marketing strategy.

Gathering Data and Insights

Throughout the market research and competitor analysis process, it is essential to gather relevant data and insights. This includes data on customer preferences, market trends, industry reports, competitor performance, and customer feedback. Various tools and resources, such as online surveys, social listening tools, analytics platforms, and market research reports, can provide valuable data and insights. Businesses should collect and analyze this information to inform their digital marketing strategies and make data-driven decisions.

By conducting thorough market research and competitor analysis, businesses gain a deep understanding of their target market, consumer behavior, and competitive landscape. Armed with these insights, they can develop digital marketing strategies that resonate with their target audience, differentiate themselves from competitors, and capitalize on market opportunities. The knowledge gained from market research and competitor analysis serves as a solid foundation for the subsequent steps in building an effective digital marketing strategy.

Identifying Target Audience and Creating Buyer Personas

In this chapter, we delve into the process of identifying the target audience and creating buyer personas as essential steps in building an effective digital marketing strategy. Understanding the target audience is crucial for businesses to tailor their marketing messages, select appropriate channels, and engage with potential customers effectively. By creating detailed buyer personas, businesses can develop a deep understanding of their ideal customers, their needs, preferences, and behaviors.

Understanding the Importance of Target Audience

We begin by emphasizing the significance of identifying the target audience. The target audience represents the specific group of people or businesses that the business aims to reach and serve.

Defining the target audience allows businesses to focus their marketing efforts, allocate resources effectively, and deliver personalized and relevant messaging. Understanding the target audience enables businesses to connect with potential customers on a deeper level and establish meaningful relationships.

Gathering Demographic and Psychographic Information

To create buyer personas, businesses gather demographic and psychographic information about their target audience. Demographic information includes age, gender, location, income level, occupation, and other relevant factors. Psychographic information delves into the target audience's interests, values, lifestyles, motivations, and preferences. This information helps businesses understand the psychographic makeup of their target audience, enabling them to tailor their digital marketing strategies to resonate with their specific needs and desires.

Conducting Surveys and Interviews

Surveys and interviews are effective methods for gathering information about the target audience. Businesses can create online surveys or conduct one-on-one interviews to gain insights into customer preferences, pain points, and motivations. By asking specific questions related to the business and its offerings, businesses can collect valuable data that informs the creation of buyer personas. Surveys and interviews provide direct feedback from the target audience, helping businesses understand their needs and challenges.

Analyzing Customer Data and Behavior

Analyzing customer data and behavior is another crucial aspect of identifying the target audience. By utilizing analytics tools and tracking customer interactions on websites, social media platforms, and other digital channels, businesses can gather valuable data on customer behavior, including browsing patterns, engagement levels, and purchase history. This data provides insights into the target audience's preferences, allowing businesses to customize their digital marketing strategies accordingly.

Creating Detailed Buyer Personas

Based on the gathered information, businesses can create detailed buyer personas. A buyer persona is a fictional representation of the ideal customer, incorporating demographic and psychographic characteristics. Buyer personas typically include a name, photo, job title, personal background, goals, challenges, and other relevant details. By visualizing the target audience through buyer personas, businesses can better understand their needs, preferences, and motivations, enabling them to tailor their digital marketing messages, content, and offerings to effectively engage and connect with potential customers.

Refining and Updating Buyer Personas

Buyer personas should be refined and updated periodically to reflect any changes in the target audience. As the market evolves, consumer behaviors and preferences may shift. Businesses should conduct regular research, analyze customer feedback, and monitor market trends to ensure that their buyer personas remain accurate and up to date. Refining and updating buyer personas allow businesses to adapt their digital marketing strategies to the evolving needs and expectations of their target audience.

By identifying the target audience and creating detailed buyer personas, businesses gain a deeper understanding of their ideal customers. This understanding enables them to develop tailored digital marketing strategies, select appropriate channels, and deliver personalized messaging that resonates with the target audience. The creation of buyer personas serves as a foundation for the subsequent steps in building an effective digital marketing strategy, ensuring that businesses can effectively engage and connect with their target audience and drive meaningful results.

Choosing the Right Digital Marketing Channels

In this chapter, we explore the process of choosing the right digital marketing channels as a crucial step in building an effective digital marketing strategy. With numerous digital channels available, businesses need to identify the platforms that align with their target audience, business objectives, and marketing goals. By selecting the most relevant channels, businesses can effectively reach and engage their target audience, maximizing their digital marketing efforts.

Understanding Different Digital Marketing Channels

We begin by providing an overview of the various digital marketing channels available. These channels encompass a wide range of platforms and tactics, including search engine marketing (SEM), social media marketing, email marketing, content marketing, influencer marketing, display advertising, and more. Each channel has its unique characteristics, advantages, and audience demographics. Understanding the different channels helps businesses make informed decisions regarding which ones to leverage for their digital marketing strategies.

Defining Target Audience Preferences

To choose the right digital marketing channels, businesses need to have a clear understanding of their target audience's preferences and behaviors. Conducting market research, analyzing customer data, and referring to buyer personas can provide insights into the channels that resonate most with the target audience. For example, if the target audience consists mainly of young professionals, social media platforms like Instagram or LinkedIn might be more effective in reaching and engaging them.

Aligning Channels with Business Objectives

Digital marketing channels should align with the business objectives and marketing goals. Different channels excel at achieving specific outcomes. For instance, search engine marketing (SEM) can be effective in driving website traffic and conversions, while social media marketing is well-suited for building brand awareness and fostering customer engagement. By aligning the channels with the desired outcomes, businesses ensure that their digital marketing efforts are focused and purposeful.

Considering Channel Suitability and Resources

Businesses should also consider the suitability of each channel based on their industry, resources, and capabilities. Some channels may require more extensive investments in terms of time, budget, and expertise. It is crucial to evaluate the feasibility of leveraging certain channels and ensure that the necessary resources are available to execute effective campaigns. For example, video marketing may be a powerful channel, but it requires appropriate equipment, editing capabilities, and creative expertise.

Evaluating Competitive Landscape

Analyzing the digital marketing efforts of competitors can provide valuable insights into the channels they are utilizing and their effectiveness. By monitoring competitors' activities, businesses can identify opportunities, learn from their successes and failures, and determine which channels align with their own unique value proposition. This evaluation helps businesses make informed decisions about the channels that will give them a competitive edge in the digital space.

Testing and Iterating

Digital marketing strategies should be dynamic and adaptable. Businesses can test different channels, messages, and tactics to gauge their effectiveness. Through A/B testing and data analysis, businesses can identify the channels that generate the highest engagement, conversions, and ROI. This iterative approach allows for continuous improvement and optimization of the digital marketing strategy over time.

By choosing the right digital marketing channels, businesses can effectively reach their target audience, deliver personalized messages, and achieve their marketing objectives. Understanding the different channels available, aligning them with the target audience's preferences and business objectives, considering available resources, and monitoring the competitive landscape all contribute to making informed decisions. Regular testing and optimization ensure that businesses stay ahead of trends and make data-driven adjustments for maximum impact. The strategic selection of digital marketing channels sets the stage for successful implementation of the overall digital marketing strategy.

Chapter 4
Website Optimization and User Experience

Understanding the Importance of Website Optimization and User Experience

In this chapter, we delve into the significance of website optimization and user experience in building an effective digital marketing strategy. A well-optimized website with a seamless user experience is essential for attracting, engaging, and converting visitors. By focusing on website optimization and user experience, businesses can maximize the effectiveness of their digital marketing efforts and drive desired actions from their target audience.

Website Performance Optimization

We begin by discussing website performance optimization, which involves ensuring that the website loads quickly and operates smoothly across various devices and browsers. Slow-loading websites can lead to higher bounce rates and frustration among users. We explore techniques such as optimizing image sizes, minimizing HTTP requests, and utilizing caching and content delivery networks (CDNs) to improve website speed. By prioritizing website performance, businesses can enhance user satisfaction and encourage longer browsing sessions.

Mobile Responsiveness and Adaptability

With the increasing use of mobile devices, it is crucial for businesses to optimize their websites for mobile responsiveness. We highlight the importance of responsive web design, which ensures that the website adapts seamlessly to different screen sizes and resolutions. Mobile-friendly websites provide a positive user experience, allowing users to navigate easily, read content, and interact with the website's features regardless of the device they are using. Businesses that prioritize mobile responsiveness can reach and engage a larger audience and stay ahead in the competitive digital landscape.

Intuitive Navigation and Information Architecture

An intuitive and user-friendly website navigation is essential for enhancing user experience. We discuss the significance of clear and organized navigation menus, logical page hierarchy, and easily accessible search functionality. By providing users with a seamless and intuitive navigation experience, businesses can help visitors find the information they are looking for quickly and effortlessly. Well-structured information architecture ensures that users can navigate through the website easily, increasing engagement and reducing bounce rates.

Compelling and Relevant Content

Compelling and relevant content is a key driver of user engagement and conversions. We explore the importance of creating high-quality, informative, and engaging content that resonates with the target audience. Businesses should craft content that addresses their audience's pain points, provides valuable insights, and showcases their expertise. By delivering content that meets users' needs and expectations, businesses can establish credibility, build trust, and encourage visitors to take desired actions, such as making a purchase, subscribing to a newsletter, or filling out a contact form.

Conversion Rate Optimization

Conversion rate optimization (CRO) focuses on improving the rate at which website visitors convert into customers or take desired actions. We discuss techniques such as implementing clear and compelling call-to-action buttons, optimizing landing pages, and conducting A/B testing to identify the most effective elements and designs. By continually analyzing user behavior, tracking conversion metrics, and making data-driven optimizations, businesses can enhance the conversion rate and maximize the ROI of their digital marketing efforts.

Usability Testing and Continuous Improvement

Lastly, we emphasize the importance of usability testing and continuous improvement. Usability testing involves gathering feedback from users to identify pain points, areas of confusion, or opportunities for enhancement. By conducting usability tests, businesses can make informed decisions and implement changes that improve the overall user experience. Additionally, a culture of continuous improvement ensures that the website evolves with user needs, industry trends, and technological advancements. Regular monitoring, analysis, and optimization based on user feedback and data insights help businesses deliver an exceptional user experience and maintain a competitive edge.

By focusing on website optimization and user experience, businesses can create a compelling and user-friendly online presence. A well-optimized website that provides a seamless and engaging experience across devices increases user satisfaction, encourages longer engagement, and drives conversions. By prioritizing website performance, mobile responsiveness, intuitive navigation, compelling content, conversion rate optimization, and continuous improvement, businesses can create a website that not only attracts visitors but also delivers a positive and impactful user experience.

Designing a User-Friendly Website

In this chapter, we delve into the process of designing a user-friendly website, which is essential for providing visitors with a positive experience and maximizing the effectiveness of digital marketing efforts. A user-friendly website ensures that visitors can navigate, engage, and find information easily, leading to increased engagement, conversions, and customer satisfaction.

Clear and Intuitive Navigation

We begin by emphasizing the importance of clear and intuitive navigation. A well-designed navigation menu enables visitors to find the information they are looking for quickly and effortlessly. We discuss techniques such as organizing navigation items logically, using descriptive labels, and providing breadcrumbs to help users understand their current location within the website's structure. By simplifying navigation and reducing friction, businesses can enhance user experience and encourage visitors to explore further.

Responsive and Mobile-Friendly Design

With the increasing use of mobile devices, it is crucial to design websites that are responsive and mobile-friendly. We explore the significance of responsive web design, which ensures that the website adapts seamlessly to different screen sizes and resolutions. By optimizing the website's layout, font sizes, and interactive elements for mobile devices, businesses can provide a consistent and enjoyable user experience across all platforms. Mobile-friendly design not only improves user satisfaction but also boosts search engine rankings, as search engines prioritize mobile-friendly websites in their results.

Readable and Engaging Content

Readable and engaging content is a key component of a user-friendly website. We discuss the importance of using clear and legible fonts, appropriate font sizes, and sufficient line spacing to enhance readability. Businesses should also focus on creating concise and scannable content, utilizing headings, bullet points, and visuals to break up text and improve comprehension. By presenting information in a visually appealing and easily digestible manner, businesses can keep visitors engaged and encourage them to spend more time on the website.

Consistent Branding and Visual Design

Consistent branding and visual design contribute to a cohesive and professional user experience. We explore the significance of incorporating consistent branding elements, such as logos, color schemes, and typography, throughout the website. Consistency in design elements helps build brand recognition and fosters a sense of trust and familiarity among visitors. By maintaining a visually appealing and coherent design, businesses can enhance the overall user experience and reinforce their brand identity.

Optimized Page Loading Speed

Page loading speed plays a crucial role in user experience and website performance. We discuss techniques such as optimizing image sizes, minimizing server response time, and leveraging browser caching to improve page loading speed. A fast-loading website reduces bounce rates and keeps visitors engaged, as they do not have to wait for content to appear. By prioritizing page speed optimization, businesses can provide a seamless and efficient browsing experience, enhancing user satisfaction and encouraging repeat visits.

User-Friendly Forms and Calls to Action

User-friendly forms and calls to action are essential for facilitating conversions and capturing visitor information. We explore best practices for designing forms that are easy to complete, with clear labels and appropriate input fields. Businesses should also optimize calls to action (CTAs) by making them visually prominent, using compelling copy, and ensuring they stand out on the page. By simplifying the conversion process and making it user-friendly, businesses can increase the likelihood of visitors taking desired actions.

User Testing and Feedback

Throughout the website design process, user testing and feedback play a crucial role in identifying areas for improvement and enhancing the user experience. We discuss the importance of conducting usability tests, gathering feedback from real users, and incorporating their insights into website design iterations. By actively involving users in the design process, businesses can uncover usability issues, optimize user flow, and deliver a website that aligns with user needs and expectations.

By focusing on designing a user-friendly website, businesses can create a positive and engaging online experience for visitors. Clear and intuitive navigation, responsive design, readable content, consistent branding, optimized page loading speed, user-friendly forms and calls to action, and user testing all contribute to a website that is easy to use and delivers a seamless user experience. By prioritizing user-centric design principles, businesses can increase engagement, conversions, and customer satisfaction, ultimately driving the success of their digital marketing efforts.

Implementing Search Engine Optimization (SEO) Techniques

In this chapter, we explore the importance of implementing search engine optimization (SEO) techniques as part of website optimization. SEO plays a critical role in improving website visibility, driving organic traffic, and enhancing the overall user experience. By implementing effective SEO strategies, businesses can increase their online presence, attract relevant visitors, and achieve higher rankings in search engine results pages (SERPs).

Keyword Research and Optimization

We begin by discussing the significance of keyword research in SEO. Keyword research involves identifying the search terms and phrases that potential customers use when searching for products, services, or information related to the business. By conducting thorough keyword research, businesses can uncover valuable insights into user intent and behavior. Optimizing website content, including headings, titles, meta descriptions, and on-page content, with relevant keywords helps search engines understand the website's relevance to user queries.

On-Page Optimization

On-page optimization focuses on optimizing individual web pages to improve their visibility and relevance to search engines. We explore techniques such as optimizing meta tags, URL structure, headings, and image alt tags. By adhering to on-page optimization best practices, businesses can improve their website's crawlability and indexability, making it easier for search engines to understand and rank the content.

Technical SEO

Technical SEO involves optimizing the technical aspects of a website to ensure search engines can effectively crawl, index, and understand the content. We discuss techniques such as XML sitemaps, robots.txt files, canonical tags, and schema markup. Implementing technical SEO practices helps search engines interpret website content accurately and improves overall website performance, which positively impacts search rankings.

Website Architecture and Structure

Website architecture and structure play a crucial role in both user experience and SEO. We discuss the importance of organizing content into logical categories, creating a clear and intuitive navigation structure, and implementing internal linking strategies. A well-structured website not only enhances user navigation but also enables search engines to crawl and understand the website's content hierarchy and relevance.

Content Optimization

Content optimization focuses on creating high-quality, informative, and relevant content that aligns with user intent and search engine guidelines. We explore techniques such as incorporating targeted keywords naturally, optimizing content length and readability, and utilizing header tags and bullet points. By optimizing website content, businesses can improve search engine visibility, attract organic traffic, and provide valuable information to users.

Mobile Optimization

Mobile optimization is critical, considering the increasing use of mobile devices for internet browsing. We discuss the importance of responsive web design, fast page loading speed, and mobile-friendly user interfaces. Mobile optimization ensures that websites provide a seamless and user-friendly experience across different devices, enhancing both user satisfaction and search engine rankings.

Link Building and Off-Page SEO

Link building and off-page SEO techniques are vital for establishing website authority and credibility. We explore strategies such as acquiring high-quality backlinks from reputable websites, engaging in social media promotion, and fostering relationships with industry influencers. Effective link building efforts enhance the website's reputation and visibility, signaling to search engines that the website offers valuable content and deserves higher rankings.

Regular Monitoring and Analysis

Regular monitoring and analysis are essential to measure the effectiveness of SEO strategies and make data-driven optimizations. We discuss the importance of monitoring key performance indicators (KPIs) such as organic traffic, rankings, bounce rates, and conversions. By leveraging analytics tools and staying informed about search engine algorithm updates, businesses can identify areas for improvement, refine their SEO strategies, and stay ahead in search engine rankings.

By implementing effective SEO techniques, businesses can improve their website's visibility, attract organic traffic, and enhance the overall user experience. Keyword research and optimization, on-page and technical SEO, website architecture and structure, content optimization, mobile optimization, link building and off-page SEO, and regular monitoring and analysis all contribute to a comprehensive SEO strategy. By continuously optimizing their websites for search engines, businesses can increase their online presence, reach their target audience, and achieve sustainable growth.

Enhancing Website Performance and Mobile Optimization

In this chapter, we explore the importance of enhancing website performance and mobile optimization as integral parts of website optimization and user experience. A fast-loading, responsive website not only improves user satisfaction but also contributes to better search engine rankings and increased conversions. By focusing on website performance and mobile optimization, businesses can deliver a seamless and engaging experience to their audience across various devices.

Optimizing Page Loading Speed

We begin by discussing the significance of optimizing page loading speed. Slow-loading websites can lead to high bounce rates and frustrated visitors. We explore techniques such as optimizing image sizes, minifying code and scripts, leveraging browser caching, and utilizing content delivery networks (CDNs). By implementing these optimization practices, businesses can improve website loading times, providing a smooth and efficient browsing experience that keeps visitors engaged and encourages them to explore further.

Responsive Web Design

With the rise of mobile browsing, responsive web design has become crucial for delivering a consistent and user-friendly experience across different devices and screen sizes. We delve into the importance of designing websites that automatically adapt to various resolutions and orientations. Responsive design ensures that website elements, content, and functionality remain accessible and visually appealing, regardless of the device being used. By prioritizing responsive web design, businesses can cater to the growing mobile audience and provide a seamless experience on smartphones and tablets.

Mobile-Friendly User Interface

Mobile optimization extends beyond responsive design. We discuss the significance of creating a mobile-friendly user interface that is specifically tailored to the unique characteristics of mobile devices. This includes designing touch-friendly buttons and menus, using appropriate font sizes and spacing for mobile screens, and simplifying forms and navigation for ease of use on smaller screens. By optimizing the user interface for mobile devices, businesses can ensure that mobile users have a positive and intuitive experience, leading to increased engagement and conversions.

Accelerated Mobile Pages (AMP)

Accelerated Mobile Pages (AMP) is a technology that further enhances mobile optimization by delivering ultra-fast loading times for mobile web pages. We explore the benefits of implementing AMP, such as improved user experience, reduced bounce rates, and enhanced visibility in mobile search results. By creating AMP versions of relevant web pages, businesses can provide an exceptional mobile browsing experience, particularly for content-focused pages like articles, blog posts, and news updates.

Streamlining and Optimizing Website Code

The efficiency of website code significantly impacts performance. We discuss the importance of streamlining and optimizing website code to reduce unnecessary scripts, CSS, and HTML. By minifying code, eliminating render-blocking resources, and compressing files, businesses can improve website loading speed and overall performance. Clean and optimized code ensures that web pages are delivered quickly and efficiently, enhancing user experience and search engine visibility.

Testing and Optimization Across Devices

To ensure a seamless experience on various devices, businesses should conduct thorough testing and optimization. We emphasize the importance of testing websites on different screen sizes, operating systems, and browsers. By identifying and addressing any usability or display issues, businesses can provide a consistent and high-quality user experience across the diverse landscape of devices used by their audience.

Continuous Monitoring and Improvement

Website performance and mobile optimization require ongoing monitoring and continuous improvement. We discuss the importance of utilizing analytics tools to track key performance indicators (KPIs), such as page loading speed, bounce rates, and user engagement on different devices. By regularly analyzing data, identifying areas for improvement, and implementing iterative changes, businesses can ensure their website remains fast, user-friendly, and optimized for mobile devices.

By enhancing website performance and implementing mobile optimization strategies, businesses can provide a seamless and engaging user experience across devices. Optimizing page loading speed, embracing responsive web design, creating mobile-friendly user interfaces, utilizing AMP, streamlining website code, conducting testing and optimization, and continuously monitoring and improving performance all contribute to an exceptional user experience. By prioritizing website performance and mobile optimization, businesses can increase user satisfaction, drive conversions, and stay ahead in the competitive digital landscape.

Chapter 5
Content Marketing and Storytelling

In this chapter, we delve into the power of content marketing and storytelling as effective strategies for engaging audiences and driving business success. Content marketing involves creating and sharing valuable, relevant, and consistent content to attract and retain a clearly defined target audience. By incorporating storytelling techniques, businesses can create a compelling narrative that captivates their audience and builds strong emotional connections.

Understanding Content Marketing

We begin by exploring the concept of content marketing and its importance in today's digital landscape. Content marketing goes beyond traditional advertising and focuses on providing valuable information, entertainment, or education to the target audience. We discuss the benefits of content marketing, such as establishing thought leadership, building brand awareness, nurturing customer relationships, and driving conversions. By delivering valuable content, businesses can position themselves as trusted authorities in their industry and gain the attention and loyalty of their target audience.

Creating Engaging and Relevant Content

We emphasize the significance of creating engaging and relevant content that resonates with the target audience. We discuss various types of content, including blog articles, videos, infographics, podcasts, and social media posts. Businesses should understand their audience's preferences and pain points to develop content that addresses their needs and interests. By crafting high-quality and valuable content, businesses can attract and engage their audience, positioning themselves as a go-to resource for information and solutions.

Telling Compelling Stories

Storytelling is a powerful technique for connecting with audiences on an emotional level. We explore the elements of effective storytelling, including developing relatable characters, creating a compelling plot, and evoking emotions. By incorporating storytelling into content marketing efforts, businesses can engage and captivate their audience, creating memorable experiences that leave a lasting impression. Stories have the power to inspire, entertain, and educate, making them an effective tool for building brand loyalty and driving customer engagement.

Aligning Content with Brand Identity

We discuss the importance of aligning content with the brand's identity and values. Consistency in messaging, tone, and style helps reinforce the brand's personality and resonates with the target audience. We explore techniques for infusing brand elements into content, such as using brand voice, incorporating brand visuals, and showcasing brand values through storytelling. By ensuring that content aligns with the brand identity, businesses can strengthen their brand perception and foster a sense of authenticity and trust among their audience.

Leveraging Content Distribution Channels

Creating great content is only half the battle; businesses must also effectively distribute it to reach their target audience. We discuss various content distribution channels, including social media platforms, email marketing, influencer collaborations, and search engine optimization (SEO). Each channel requires a tailored approach to maximize visibility and engagement. By leveraging the right distribution channels, businesses can amplify their content's reach, attract new audiences, and drive traffic to their website.

Measuring Content Performance and Iterating

Measuring the performance of content marketing efforts is crucial for optimizing strategies and achieving desired outcomes. We explore key performance indicators (KPIs) such as website traffic, engagement metrics, social media reach, and conversion rates. By utilizing analytics tools and analyzing data, businesses can gain insights into what content resonates best with their audience and make data-driven decisions for future content creation. Continuous monitoring and iterating based on performance insights allow businesses to refine their content marketing strategies and drive even better results.

By incorporating content marketing and storytelling into their strategies, businesses can connect with their audience on a deeper level, build brand loyalty, and drive engagement and conversions. Creating engaging and relevant content, telling compelling stories, aligning content with brand identity, leveraging distribution channels, and measuring content performance all contribute to a successful content marketing strategy. By consistently delivering valuable content and engaging narratives, businesses can establish themselves as trusted authorities and nurture long-lasting relationships with their target audience.

Crafting Compelling and Relevant Content

In this chapter, we explore the art of crafting compelling and relevant content as a fundamental aspect of content marketing. Engaging and valuable content is the cornerstone of attracting and retaining an audience, driving brand awareness, and ultimately achieving business success. By understanding the needs and interests of the target audience, businesses can create content that resonates with their audience and establishes them as a trusted source of information and solutions.

Understanding the Target Audience

We begin by emphasizing the importance of understanding the target audience. By conducting market research, analyzing demographics, and identifying buyer personas, businesses gain insights into their audience's preferences, pain points, and interests. This understanding forms the foundation for creating content that speaks directly to their needs and captures their attention. By tailoring content to the specific interests and challenges of the target audience, businesses can position themselves as valuable resources and build strong connections.

Providing Value and Solving Problems

Valuable content is key to capturing and retaining the audience's attention. We discuss the significance of providing educational, informative, and entertaining content that addresses the audience's problems or provides solutions. By offering insights, tips, tutorials, or expert advice, businesses can establish themselves as industry leaders and go-to sources of relevant information. Valuable content not only builds trust but also encourages the audience to engage, share, and return for more.

Storytelling and Emotion

Storytelling is a powerful technique for creating emotional connections with the audience. We explore the elements of storytelling, such as character development, conflict, and resolution. By incorporating storytelling into content, businesses can evoke emotions, captivate the audience, and make a lasting impact. Stories have the ability to inspire, entertain, and engage on a deeper level, allowing businesses to forge meaningful connections and foster brand loyalty.

Visual and Interactive Content

Visual and interactive content can significantly enhance engagement and make content more memorable. We discuss the effectiveness of using images, videos, infographics, and interactive elements to capture the audience's attention and convey information in a compelling way. Visual content not only breaks up the text but also helps convey complex concepts quickly and effectively. Interactive content, such as quizzes, surveys, and interactive infographics, encourages audience participation and creates a more immersive experience.

Consistency and Freshness

Consistency is key to maintaining audience engagement and building a loyal following. We emphasize the importance of delivering content consistently and adhering to a content calendar or publishing schedule. Regularly updating content demonstrates the business's commitment to providing up-to-date and relevant information. Additionally, businesses should strive to create fresh and unique content that offers a fresh perspective or presents information in a new and interesting way. By staying current and innovative, businesses can attract and retain their audience's attention.

Engaging Headlines and Hooks

Capturing the audience's attention starts with engaging headlines and hooks. We explore techniques for crafting compelling headlines that pique curiosity and entice readers to click and explore further. Businesses should focus on creating clear, concise, and intriguing headlines that convey the value and relevance of the content. Hooks, such as compelling introductions or opening statements, help captivate the audience from the start and compel them to continue reading or engaging with the content.

User-Generated Content and Social Proof

User-generated content and social proof play a significant role in building trust and authenticity. We discuss the benefits of encouraging user-generated content, such as customer testimonials, reviews, and user-contributed stories. By showcasing real experiences and positive feedback, businesses can leverage social proof to establish credibility and inspire confidence in their audience. User-generated content also fosters a sense of community and encourages audience participation.

By crafting compelling and relevant content, businesses can captivate their audience, establish thought leadership, and drive engagement and conversions. Understanding the target audience, providing value, incorporating storytelling and emotion, leveraging visual and interactive elements, maintaining consistency and freshness, creating engaging headlines and hooks, and leveraging user-generated content all contribute to a robust content marketing strategy. By consistently delivering high-quality content that meets the audience's needs and interests, businesses can build strong connections, foster brand loyalty, and achieve long-term success.

Implementing Content Distribution Strategies

In this chapter, we explore the importance of implementing effective content distribution strategies as a crucial component of content marketing. Creating great content is only half the battle; businesses must also ensure that their content reaches the target audience and generates maximum visibility and engagement. By leveraging various content distribution channels and tactics, businesses can amplify their content's reach, attract new audiences, and drive traffic to their website.

Understanding Content Distribution Channels

We begin by discussing the different content distribution channels available. These channels encompass a wide range of platforms and tactics, including social media platforms, email marketing, influencer collaborations, guest blogging, content syndication, and search engine optimization (SEO). Each channel offers unique advantages and audience reach, and businesses should carefully select the channels that align with their target audience's preferences and behaviors.

Social Media Marketing

Social media platforms are powerful tools for content distribution. We explore the significance of selecting the right social media channels based on the target audience demographics and interests. Businesses should create engaging and shareable content that resonates with the social media users. By leveraging social media marketing techniques such as creating compelling visuals, using appropriate hashtags, and encouraging audience participation, businesses can increase content visibility, generate social shares, and drive website traffic.

Email Marketing

Email marketing is an effective content distribution strategy for reaching a targeted audience directly. We discuss the importance of building an email list and segmenting it based on user interests. By crafting personalized and relevant email campaigns that deliver valuable content, businesses can nurture relationships with their subscribers, drive traffic to specific pieces of content, and encourage engagement and conversions.

Influencer Collaborations

Collaborating with influencers can significantly expand the reach and visibility of content. We explore the benefits of identifying influencers in the industry or niche and partnering with them to promote content to their audience. By leveraging the influencer's credibility and following, businesses can tap into new audiences, gain social proof, and drive traffic to their content.

Guest Blogging

Guest blogging involves writing and publishing content on external websites or blogs. We discuss the advantages of guest blogging, such as reaching new audiences, building backlinks, and establishing thought leadership. By identifying reputable websites that align with the target audience's interests, businesses can contribute valuable content and gain exposure to a broader readership.

Content Syndication

Content syndication involves distributing content through third-party platforms or networks. We explore the benefits of syndicating content on platforms such as Medium, LinkedIn Pulse, or industry-specific content aggregators. Syndication allows businesses to reach wider audiences, increase brand visibility, and drive traffic back to their website.

Search Engine Optimization (SEO)

Search engine optimization (SEO) plays a crucial role in content distribution by improving the visibility of content in search engine results pages (SERPs). We discuss the importance of optimizing content for relevant keywords, creating meta tags and descriptions, and building high-quality backlinks. By implementing effective SEO strategies, businesses can increase organic traffic to their content and attract users actively searching for relevant information.

Paid Advertising

Paid advertising offers opportunities for targeted content promotion. We explore options such as search engine advertising (pay-per-click), social media advertising, and native advertising. By strategically allocating advertising budgets and targeting specific audience segments, businesses can amplify the reach of their content, generate website traffic, and increase brand visibility.

Monitoring and Analytics

Monitoring the performance of content distribution efforts is vital to understand what channels and tactics are most effective. We discuss the importance of leveraging analytics tools to track key performance indicators (KPIs), such as website traffic, engagement metrics, conversion rates, and social shares. By analyzing data, businesses can make data-driven decisions, optimize content distribution strategies, and allocate resources to channels that deliver the best results.

By implementing effective content distribution strategies, businesses can ensure that their content reaches the target audience, generates visibility, and drives engagement and conversions. Leveraging social media marketing, email marketing, influencer collaborations, guest blogging, content syndication, SEO, paid advertising, and monitoring analytics all contribute to a comprehensive content distribution plan. By selecting the right channels and tactics based on audience preferences and behaviors, businesses can maximize the impact of their content and achieve their content marketing goals.

Chapter 6
Social Media Marketing

In this chapter, we delve into the power of social media marketing as a vital component of digital marketing strategies. Social media platforms have revolutionized communication and transformed the way businesses connect with their audience. By leveraging social media effectively, businesses can enhance brand visibility, engage with customers, drive website traffic, and foster meaningful relationships.

Understanding the Role of Social Media Marketing

We begin by discussing the significance of social media marketing in today's digital landscape. Social media platforms offer businesses a direct line of communication with their target audience, allowing them to build brand awareness, share valuable content, and engage in meaningful conversations. We explore the benefits of social media marketing, such as increasing brand visibility, expanding reach, and humanizing the brand by creating authentic connections with customers.

Selecting the Right Social Media Platforms

Not all social media platforms are created equal, and it's crucial for businesses to identify the platforms that align with their target audience's preferences and behaviors. We discuss popular platforms such as Facebook, Instagram, Twitter, LinkedIn, YouTube, and Pinterest, highlighting their unique characteristics and audience demographics. By selecting the right platforms, businesses can focus their efforts on channels that have the greatest potential to reach and engage their target audience effectively.

Creating Engaging Content for Social Media

Creating engaging content is key to capturing the attention and interest of social media users. We explore various types of content, including images, videos, infographics, live streams, and interactive content. Businesses should focus on delivering valuable, entertaining, and visually appealing content that resonates with their target audience. By tailoring content to the preferences and interests of social media users, businesses can foster engagement, encourage social sharing, and expand their reach.

Building and Nurturing a Social Media Community

Social media provides an opportunity to build a community of loyal followers and advocates. We discuss strategies for fostering engagement, such as responding to comments and messages, asking questions, running contests or giveaways, and encouraging user-generated content. By actively engaging with followers, businesses can build strong relationships, gain valuable feedback, and create a sense of belonging and loyalty within the social media community.

Utilizing Social Media Advertising

Social media advertising offers powerful targeting options to reach specific audience segments. We explore the benefits of social media advertising platforms, such as Facebook Ads, Instagram Ads, Twitter Ads, and LinkedIn Ads. Businesses can leverage paid advertising to amplify their reach, drive website traffic, promote specific products or services, and generate leads. By developing strategic ad campaigns, businesses can maximize the impact of their social media marketing efforts.

Monitoring and Measuring Social Media Performance

Monitoring and measuring social media performance is crucial for optimizing strategies and achieving desired outcomes. We discuss the importance of tracking key metrics such as reach, engagement, follower growth, click-through rates, and conversions. By utilizing social media analytics tools and analyzing data, businesses can gain insights into the effectiveness of their social media efforts, identify trends, and make data-driven decisions to improve performance.

Staying Up-to-Date with Social Media Trends

Social media is a dynamic and ever-changing landscape. We emphasize the significance of staying informed about the latest social media trends, features, and algorithm updates. By adapting to emerging trends and embracing new features, businesses can stay ahead of the curve, capture audience attention, and maintain a competitive edge in their social media marketing strategies.

By harnessing the power of social media marketing, businesses can strengthen their brand presence, engage with their audience on a personal level, and drive meaningful interactions. Selecting the right platforms, creating engaging content, building a social media community, utilizing advertising opportunities, monitoring performance, and staying updated with trends all contribute to a comprehensive social media marketing strategy. By leveraging social media effectively, businesses can achieve their marketing objectives and thrive in the digital landscape.

Developing a Social Media Strategy

In this chapter, we explore the process of developing an effective social media strategy that aligns with business goals and maximizes the impact of social media marketing efforts. A well-crafted social media strategy provides a roadmap for businesses to leverage social media platforms to achieve their objectives, engage with their audience, and drive meaningful results.

Defining Goals and Objectives

We begin by emphasizing the importance of defining clear and specific goals and objectives for the social media strategy. Whether it's increasing brand awareness, driving website traffic, generating leads, or improving customer engagement, businesses should identify what they aim to achieve through their social media efforts. Clear goals provide direction and serve as a benchmark for measuring success.

Understanding the Target Audience

A deep understanding of the target audience is crucial in developing an effective social media strategy. We discuss the significance of conducting audience research, analyzing demographics, interests, behaviors, and pain points. By gaining insights into their audience's preferences, businesses can tailor their content, messaging, and engagement strategies to resonate with their target audience effectively.

Selecting the Right Social Media Platforms

We delve into the process of selecting the right social media platforms based on the target audience's preferences and behaviors. Each platform has its own unique characteristics, user demographics, and engagement patterns. Businesses should evaluate platforms such as Facebook, Instagram, Twitter, LinkedIn, YouTube, and Pinterest, and choose the ones that align with their target audience and support their goals.

Creating a Content Strategy

A well-defined content strategy is key to engaging the target audience and driving social media success. We discuss the importance of creating valuable, relevant, and shareable content that aligns with the target audience's interests and needs. Businesses should determine content themes, formats, and posting frequency, while also considering how to leverage user-generated content and storytelling techniques to enhance engagement.

Developing a Brand Voice and Tone

Consistency in brand voice and tone is essential for building a strong brand identity on social media. We explore the process of defining a brand voice that reflects the business's personality, values, and positioning. By establishing guidelines for social media communication, businesses can maintain a consistent tone that resonates with their target audience and strengthens brand recognition.

Engaging and Community Building

Engagement is a vital aspect of social media strategy. We discuss techniques for fostering meaningful interactions with the audience, including responding to comments, messages, and mentions, asking questions, running contests or polls, and encouraging user-generated content. By actively engaging with the audience, businesses can build a loyal community, foster brand advocacy, and drive word-of-mouth marketing.

Leveraging Social Media Advertising

We explore the role of social media advertising in amplifying social media efforts. Businesses should consider paid advertising options on platforms like Facebook Ads, Instagram Ads, Twitter Ads, or LinkedIn Ads to reach a wider audience, promote specific content or offerings, and drive targeted traffic to their website. By setting clear objectives, defining target audiences, and optimizing ad campaigns, businesses can maximize the impact of their social media advertising.

Monitoring, Measuring, and Iterating

Monitoring and measuring social media performance are essential for evaluating the effectiveness of the strategy. We discuss the importance of tracking key metrics such as reach, engagement, follower growth, click-through rates, and conversions. By leveraging social media analytics tools and analyzing data, businesses can gain insights into what works and make data-driven optimizations to improve performance continually.

Staying Updated and Evolving

Social media is dynamic, and it's crucial for businesses to stay updated with the latest trends, features, and changes in algorithms. We emphasize the importance of continuous learning, adapting strategies based on audience behavior and platform updates, and embracing new opportunities. By staying informed and evolving with the social media landscape, businesses can remain competitive and maximize their social media marketing potential.

By developing a well-crafted social media strategy, businesses can effectively harness the power of social media platforms to achieve their goals, engage with their target audience, and drive meaningful results. Defining goals, understanding the target audience, selecting the right platforms, creating a content strategy, developing a brand voice, fostering engagement, leveraging social media advertising, monitoring performance, and staying updated all contribute to a comprehensive social media strategy that delivers tangible business outcomes.

Engaging with Followers and Building Brand Loyalty

In this chapter, we explore the importance of engaging with followers on social media and building brand loyalty through meaningful interactions. Social media platforms provide businesses with a unique opportunity to connect directly with their audience, foster relationships, and create a loyal community of brand advocates.

Listening and Responding to Feedback

Listening to the audience and responding to their feedback is key to building engagement and loyalty. We discuss the significance of actively monitoring comments, messages, and mentions on social media and promptly responding to inquiries, concerns, or compliments. By demonstrating attentiveness and addressing audience feedback, businesses can show that they value their followers' opinions and are committed to providing excellent customer service.

Asking Questions and Encouraging Conversations

Engaging with followers involves initiating conversations and encouraging active participation. We explore techniques such as asking open-ended questions, running polls or surveys, and seeking input on relevant topics. By inviting followers to share their thoughts, experiences, and ideas, businesses can create a sense of community and make followers feel valued. Meaningful conversations not only strengthen the connection between the brand and its followers but also provide valuable insights for business improvements.

Sharing User-Generated Content

User-generated content (UGC) is a powerful tool for building brand loyalty. We discuss the benefits of sharing and showcasing UGC, such as customer testimonials, reviews, photos, or videos. By featuring UGC on social media platforms, businesses can demonstrate that they appreciate and value their customers, while also encouraging others to engage and contribute their own content. UGC fosters a sense of belonging and strengthens the bond between the brand and its community.

Running Contests and Giveaways

Contests and giveaways are effective strategies for engaging followers and creating excitement. We explore the benefits of running social media contests or giveaways, where participants have the opportunity to win prizes by engaging with the brand's content, sharing posts, or submitting user-generated content. Such activities generate buzz, encourage participation, and increase brand visibility. By rewarding followers and creating a sense of anticipation, businesses can drive engagement and loyalty.

Providing Valuable and Shareable Content

Delivering valuable and shareable content is fundamental to engaging followers and building brand loyalty. We discuss the importance of creating content that educates, entertains, or solves problems for the target audience. By consistently offering content that adds value to followers' lives, businesses can position themselves as a trusted resource and encourage social sharing. Valuable and shareable content not only increases brand reach but also fosters a sense of loyalty as followers identify the brand as a reliable and helpful source.

Personalizing Interactions

Personalization is key to building strong relationships and loyalty on social media. We explore techniques such as addressing followers by name, acknowledging milestones or special occasions, and tailoring content to specific audience segments. By personalizing interactions, businesses demonstrate that they see followers as individuals and care about their unique needs. Personalization creates a sense of connection and enhances the overall user experience on social media.

Rewarding Loyalty

Recognizing and rewarding loyal followers is crucial for building brand loyalty. We discuss strategies such as exclusive offers, discounts, or early access to new products or content for loyal followers. By showing appreciation for their support, businesses can foster a sense of exclusivity and make followers feel valued and special. Loyalty rewards reinforce positive brand associations and encourage continued engagement and advocacy.

By engaging with followers on social media and building brand loyalty, businesses can create a passionate community of brand advocates who not only support the brand but also actively promote it to others. By listening and responding to feedback, encouraging conversations, sharing user-generated content, running contests, providing valuable content, personalizing interactions, and rewarding loyalty, businesses can cultivate a loyal following that forms the foundation for long-term success on social media.

Leveraging Social Media Advertising

In this chapter, we explore the power of social media advertising as a strategic tool to enhance social media marketing efforts and achieve specific business objectives. Social media advertising offers businesses the ability to reach highly targeted audiences, increase brand visibility, drive website traffic, and generate leads. By leveraging social media advertising effectively, businesses can maximize their return on investment and achieve their marketing goals.

Understanding Social Media Advertising Platforms

We begin by discussing the various social media advertising platforms available, such as Facebook Ads, Instagram Ads, Twitter Ads, LinkedIn Ads, and Pinterest Ads. We explore the unique features, targeting options, and ad formats offered by each platform. Understanding the capabilities of different platforms allows businesses to choose the most suitable ones based on their target audience and campaign objectives.

Defining Advertising Objectives

Clarifying advertising objectives is essential for a successful social media advertising campaign. We discuss common objectives such as increasing brand awareness, driving website traffic, generating leads, promoting products or services, or increasing conversions. By clearly defining objectives, businesses can align their ad campaigns with specific goals and track the success of their advertising efforts.

Identifying Target Audiences

Effective social media advertising relies on precise targeting. We explore the importance of identifying and understanding target audiences, including demographic factors, interests, behaviors, and preferences. Social media platforms offer extensive targeting options, such as age, location, interests, job titles, and more. By defining a target audience and leveraging detailed targeting features, businesses can ensure their ads reach the most relevant users who are likely to be interested in their offerings.

Crafting Compelling Ad Creatives

Compelling ad creatives play a crucial role in capturing audience attention and driving engagement. We discuss techniques for creating attention-grabbing visuals, compelling ad copy, and clear calls-to-action. Advertisements should be visually appealing, aligned with the brand's aesthetics, and communicate the value proposition effectively. By investing in high-quality visuals and persuasive copy, businesses can increase the effectiveness of their social media ads.

Setting Budgets and Bidding Strategies

Budgeting and bidding strategies are critical for managing social media advertising campaigns effectively. We explore options such as daily or lifetime budgets and different bidding methods, such as cost per click (CPC) or cost per impression (CPM). By setting realistic budgets and selecting appropriate bidding strategies, businesses can optimize their ad spend, control costs, and maximize the reach and impact of their advertisements.

Monitoring and Optimizing Campaign Performance

Monitoring and optimizing campaign performance are essential for maximizing the effectiveness of social media advertising. We discuss the importance of regularly tracking key performance indicators (KPIs), such as click-through rates, conversion rates, cost per acquisition, and return on ad spend. By analyzing campaign data and making data-driven optimizations, businesses can refine their targeting, adjust ad creatives, and allocate budgets to campaigns that deliver the best results.

A/B Testing and Experimentation

A/B testing and experimentation are valuable strategies for optimizing social media advertising campaigns. We explore the benefits of testing different ad variations, such as visuals, headlines, or calls-to-action, to identify the most effective combinations. By conducting experiments and analyzing the results, businesses can fine-tune their ads, improve campaign performance, and gain insights into audience preferences and behaviors.

Retargeting and Remarketing

Retargeting and remarketing allow businesses to re-engage users who have previously interacted with their brand. We discuss the significance of using retargeting pixels and custom audience targeting to deliver tailored ads to users who have visited the website or shown interest in specific products or services. By staying top of mind and delivering personalized messaging, businesses can increase conversions and drive repeat engagements.

By leveraging social media advertising effectively, businesses can reach their target audience with precision, increase brand visibility, and drive desired actions. Understanding advertising platforms, defining objectives, identifying target audiences, crafting compelling ad creatives, setting budgets and bidding strategies, monitoring and optimizing campaign performance, conducting A/B testing, and utilizing retargeting and remarketing techniques all contribute to a successful social media advertising strategy.

Chapter 7
Search Engine Marketing (SEM) and Pay-Per-Click (PPC)

In this chapter, we delve into the realm of Search Engine Marketing (SEM) and Pay-Per-Click (PPC) advertising as powerful tools for driving targeted traffic, increasing brand visibility, and achieving measurable results. SEM and PPC strategies enable businesses to place ads within search engine results pages, allowing them to reach potential customers actively searching for relevant products or services.

Understanding Search Engine Marketing (SEM)

We begin by discussing the concept of Search Engine Marketing (SEM) and its importance in digital marketing strategies. SEM involves the promotion of websites through paid advertising efforts to increase visibility on search engine results pages (SERPs). We explore how search engines, such as Google, Bing, or Yahoo, serve as platforms for businesses to showcase their ads to users actively seeking information or solutions. By leveraging SEM, businesses can ensure their offerings are prominently displayed to potential customers, maximizing their chances of engagement and conversions.

Key Elements of Pay-Per-Click (PPC) Advertising

Pay-Per-Click (PPC) advertising is a fundamental component of SEM. We discuss the key elements of PPC advertising, including the auction-based model, bidding strategies, and ad rank determination.

With PPC, businesses only pay when their ads are clicked, making it a cost-effective way to drive targeted traffic. We explore how ad rank, determined by factors like bid amount, ad relevance, and landing page experience, affects the visibility and success of PPC ads.

Keyword Research and Selection

Effective keyword research and selection are critical in SEM and PPC campaigns. We emphasize the importance of identifying relevant keywords that align with business offerings and target audience search intent. We discuss the use of keyword research tools, competitor analysis, and customer insights to uncover valuable keywords. By targeting the right keywords, businesses can optimize their ads for higher relevancy, increase click-through rates, and attract qualified leads.

Creating Compelling Ad Copy

Crafting compelling ad copy is key to capturing user attention and driving click-through rates. We explore techniques for writing concise, persuasive, and engaging ad copy that communicates the unique selling propositions of the business. Businesses should focus on delivering a clear value proposition, highlighting benefits, and incorporating compelling calls-to-action. By creating compelling ad copy, businesses can differentiate themselves from competitors and entice users to click on their ads.

Landing Page Optimization

An effective landing page is crucial for converting ad clicks into desired actions, such as purchases, sign-ups, or inquiries. We discuss the elements of a well-optimized landing page, including compelling headlines, persuasive content, clear calls-to-action, and user-friendly design. Businesses should ensure that landing pages align with ad messaging, provide relevant information, and offer a seamless user experience. By optimizing landing pages, businesses can increase conversion rates and maximize the return on their PPC investments.

Monitoring, Testing, and Optimization

Continuous monitoring, testing, and optimization are essential for successful SEM and PPC campaigns. We discuss the importance of tracking key performance metrics, such as click-through rates (CTR), conversion rates, cost per acquisition (CPA), and return on ad spend (ROAS). By analyzing campaign data, businesses can identify areas for improvement, conduct A/B testing to optimize ads and landing pages, and refine their targeting and bidding strategies. Ongoing optimization ensures that SEM and PPC campaigns deliver the best possible results and maximize the overall marketing ROI.

Remarketing and Display Advertising

We explore the additional benefits of remarketing and display advertising in SEM strategies. Remarketing allows businesses to target users who have previously visited their website, offering personalized ads to re-engage them. Display advertising involves placing visually appealing ads on relevant websites within the Google Display Network or other advertising networks. By leveraging remarketing and display advertising, businesses can reinforce brand presence, increase conversions, and reach a wider audience beyond search engine results pages.

By embracing Search Engine Marketing (SEM) and Pay-Per-Click (PPC) strategies, businesses can gain a competitive edge in the digital landscape. By conducting thorough keyword research, crafting compelling ad copy, optimizing landing pages, monitoring campaign performance, and leveraging remarketing and display advertising, businesses can drive targeted traffic, increase brand visibility, and achieve measurable results through SEM and PPC advertising.

Understanding Search Engine Marketing (SEM) and its Benefits

In this chapter, we explore the concept of Search Engine Marketing (SEM) and the numerous benefits it offers to businesses. SEM involves promoting websites and increasing their visibility on search engine results pages (SERPs) through paid advertising efforts. By leveraging SEM strategies, businesses can tap into the massive user base of search engines and connect with potential customers who are actively searching for products or services.

Increased Online Visibility

One of the primary benefits of SEM is the ability to enhance online visibility. Search engines like Google, Bing, or Yahoo serve as platforms where businesses can display their ads prominently within the search results. This increased visibility ensures that businesses are more likely to be noticed by users looking for relevant information or solutions. By occupying prime positions on SERPs, businesses can capture the attention of their target audience and stand out from the competition.

Targeted Reach

SEM enables businesses to reach a highly targeted audience. Through keyword research and selection, businesses can identify the specific keywords and search terms that are relevant to their offerings and align with their target audience's search intent. By displaying ads when users search for those specific keywords, businesses can ensure that their message reaches the most relevant audience, increasing the likelihood of engagement and conversions.

Cost-Effective Advertising

SEM, particularly Pay-Per-Click (PPC) advertising, offers a cost-effective advertising model. With PPC, businesses only pay when their ads are clicked, making it a highly efficient way to drive targeted traffic to their websites. This cost structure allows businesses to allocate their budgets more effectively and optimize their ad spend by focusing on keywords and targeting options that generate the best results. The ability to measure and track campaign performance also provides valuable insights for optimizing future advertising efforts.

Measurable Results

One of the key advantages of SEM is its measurability. Businesses can track and measure various performance metrics, such as click-through rates (CTR), conversion rates, cost per acquisition (CPA), and return on ad spend (ROAS). These metrics provide valuable insights into the effectiveness of SEM campaigns and allow businesses to make data-driven decisions to optimize their strategies. By continuously monitoring and analyzing campaign performance, businesses can refine their targeting, adjust their ad copy, and allocate their budgets more effectively.

Quick and Flexible Implementation

offers the advantage of quick and flexible implementation. Unlike traditional advertising channels, which may require extensive lead times and planning, businesses can launch SEM campaigns relatively quickly. This agility allows businesses to respond rapidly to market trends, promotions, or seasonal demands. Additionally, SEM platforms provide flexibility in terms SEM of budget allocation, targeting options, and ad variations, enabling businesses to adapt their strategies as needed to maximize results.

Enhanced Brand Exposure and Credibility

By consistently appearing in search engine results through SEM, businesses can enhance their brand exposure and establish credibility. Users often perceive businesses that consistently appear in top search results as more reputable and trustworthy. The repeated exposure through SEM helps businesses reinforce their brand presence and position themselves as industry leaders or trusted providers in their respective domains.

In summary, Search Engine Marketing (SEM) offers businesses a wide range of benefits, including increased online visibility, targeted reach, cost-effective advertising, measurable results, quick implementation, and enhanced brand exposure and credibility. By leveraging SEM strategies effectively, businesses can connect with their target audience at the right moment, drive qualified traffic to their websites, and achieve their marketing goals in the highly competitive online landscape.

Creating Effective PPC Campaigns

In this chapter, we delve into the process of creating effective Pay-Per-Click (PPC) campaigns within the realm of Search Engine Marketing (SEM). PPC advertising allows businesses to display targeted ads on search engine results pages (SERPs), and mastering the art of creating impactful PPC campaigns is essential for maximizing ad performance and achieving desired outcomes.

Defining Campaign Objectives

The first step in creating a successful PPC campaign is to define clear and specific objectives. Whether the goal is to drive website traffic, increase conversions, boost brand awareness, or generate leads, clearly articulating the campaign's purpose provides a foundation for strategic decision-making and campaign optimization.

Conducting Thorough Keyword Research

Keyword research forms the backbone of PPC campaigns. It involves identifying and selecting relevant keywords that align with the target audience's search intent and business offerings. Businesses should leverage keyword research tools, competitor analysis, customer insights, and industry trends to uncover valuable keywords. By targeting the right keywords, businesses can ensure their ads appear in front of users actively searching for relevant products or services.

Crafting Compelling Ad Copy

Compelling ad copy is crucial for capturing user attention and driving click-through rates (CTR). Ad copy should be concise, persuasive, and clearly communicate the unique selling propositions of the business. Businesses should focus on creating attention-grabbing headlines, highlighting key benefits, and incorporating strong calls-to-action (CTAs). By crafting compelling ad copy that resonates with the target audience, businesses can differentiate themselves from competitors and entice users to click on their ads.

Designing Landing Pages for Conversion

The landing page plays a vital role in converting ad clicks into desired actions, such as purchases, sign-ups, or inquiries. Businesses should design landing pages that align with ad messaging, provide relevant and valuable information, and feature clear and compelling CTAs. Landing pages should have a user-friendly layout, fast loading times, and mobile responsiveness. By optimizing landing pages for conversion, businesses can enhance the user experience and increase the likelihood of desired outcomes.

Setting Budgets and Bidding Strategies

Setting appropriate budgets and bidding strategies is essential for managing PPC campaigns effectively. Businesses should determine the maximum amount they are willing to spend on ads and allocate budgets accordingly. Additionally, selecting the right bidding strategy, such as manual bidding or automated bidding, helps optimize ad placements and maximize return on investment (ROI). Regular monitoring and adjustment of budgets and bids based on performance data contribute to campaign success.

Implementing Ad Extensions

Ad extensions are additional features that enhance the visibility and performance of PPC ads. They provide users with more information, options, and opportunities to engage with the ad. Businesses should leverage ad extensions such as site links, call extensions, location extensions, and review extensions to improve ad relevancy, increase click-through rates, and provide users with valuable information.

Tracking and Analyzing Campaign Performance

Tracking and analyzing campaign performance is crucial for optimizing PPC campaigns. Businesses should utilize tracking tools and analytics platforms to monitor key performance metrics, such as CTR, conversion rates, cost per conversion, and ROI. By analyzing the data, businesses can identify underperforming areas, make data-driven optimizations, and refine their targeting, bidding strategies, ad copy, and landing page design for better campaign outcomes.

A/B Testing and Experimentation

A/B testing and experimentation allow businesses to optimize their PPC campaigns further. By testing different variations of ad copy, headlines, landing pages, or CTAs, businesses can identify the most effective combinations and refine their strategies based on user responses. Continuous testing and experimentation help businesses uncover insights, improve ad performance, and optimize campaign outcomes over time.

By following these steps and implementing best practices, businesses can create effective PPC campaigns within their SEM strategies. Defining campaign objectives, conducting thorough keyword research, crafting compelling ad copy, designing conversion-focused landing pages, setting budgets and bidding strategies, implementing ad extensions, tracking and analyzing campaign performance, and leveraging A/B testing and experimentation all contribute to the success of PPC campaigns and drive desired results.

Optimizing Ad Performance and Measuring ROI

In this chapter, we explore the crucial steps involved in optimizing ad performance and measuring return on investment (ROI) within Pay-Per-Click (PPC) campaigns. Optimizing ad performance ensures that businesses achieve the best possible results from their advertising efforts, while measuring ROI provides valuable insights into the effectiveness and profitability of PPC campaigns.

Tracking Key Performance Metrics

The foundation of optimizing ad performance is tracking and analyzing key performance metrics. Businesses should monitor metrics such as click-through rates (CTR), conversion rates, cost per conversion, average position, quality score, and return on ad spend (ROAS). By understanding how ads perform across different metrics, businesses can identify areas for improvement and make data-driven decisions to optimize their campaigns.

Refining Targeting and Bidding Strategies

Effective targeting and bidding strategies are instrumental in optimizing ad performance. Businesses should analyze data to identify high-performing target audience segments and adjust their targeting parameters accordingly. Refining targeting allows businesses to focus their ad spend on the most relevant and valuable audience, increasing the likelihood of engagement and conversions. Similarly, optimizing bidding strategies based on performance data helps businesses achieve a balance between maximizing ad exposure and managing costs.

Conducting A/B Testing and Experimentation

A/B testing and experimentation play a crucial role in optimizing ad performance. By testing different variations of ad elements such as headlines, ad copy, calls-to-action (CTAs), or landing page designs, businesses can identify the most effective combinations that resonate with their target audience. Continuous testing and experimentation enable businesses to refine their ad elements, improve click-through rates, and increase conversion rates over time.

Ad Copy and Landing Page Optimization

Optimizing ad copy and landing pages is essential for driving higher engagement and conversions. Businesses should continuously evaluate and refine their ad copy to ensure it is compelling, relevant, and aligned with the target audience's needs and preferences. Likewise, optimizing landing pages involves improving their design, layout, and user experience to enhance conversion rates. By aligning ad copy and landing pages with audience expectations and continuously optimizing them, businesses can improve ad performance and achieve higher ROI.

Ad Position and Ad Rank Optimization

Ad position and ad rank significantly impact ad performance. Businesses should strive for optimal ad positions that capture user attention and drive higher click-through rates. Optimizing ad rank involves improving factors such as ad relevance, landing page experience, and expected click-through rate. By focusing on improving these factors, businesses can improve their ad positions, increase visibility, and maximize ad performance.

Conversion Tracking and Attribution

Tracking conversions and attributing them to specific ads or campaigns is crucial for measuring ROI accurately. Businesses should implement conversion tracking mechanisms, such as conversion pixels or tags, to track user actions, such as purchases, form submissions, or sign-ups. Attribution models help determine the contribution of different ads or touchpoints in the conversion process. By understanding which ads drive the most valuable conversions, businesses can optimize their campaigns to maximize ROI.

Continuous Monitoring and Optimization

Ad performance optimization is an ongoing process. Businesses should continuously monitor campaign performance, evaluate data, and make iterative optimizations. This includes adjusting bidding strategies, refining targeting, testing new ad variations, and optimizing landing pages based on user behavior and performance metrics. Regularly reviewing and optimizing campaigns ensure that businesses stay competitive, improve ad performance, and maximize ROI.

Calculating Return on Investment (ROI)

Measuring ROI is essential for evaluating the profitability of PPC campaigns. ROI is calculated by comparing the total revenue generated from the campaigns to the total costs, including ad spend and associated expenses. By accurately measuring ROI, businesses can determine the effectiveness of their PPC campaigns and make informed decisions regarding budget allocation and campaign adjustments.

By implementing these optimization strategies and measuring ROI, businesses can ensure their PPC campaigns deliver optimal results and provide a positive return on investment. Tracking key performance metrics, refining targeting and bidding strategies, conducting A/B testing, optimizing ad copy and landing pages, improving ad position and rank, implementing conversion tracking and attribution, continuous monitoring, and calculating ROI all contribute to optimizing ad performance and maximizing the effectiveness of PPC campaigns.

Chapter 8
Email Marketing and Automation

In this chapter, we explore the power of email marketing and automation as effective strategies for engaging with customers, nurturing leads, and driving conversions. Email marketing allows businesses to communicate directly with their audience, deliver targeted messages, and build long-term relationships. Automation takes email marketing to the next level by streamlining processes and delivering personalized, timely content to subscribers.

Understanding Email Marketing

We begin by discussing the fundamentals of email marketing and its benefits. Email marketing involves sending targeted messages to a subscriber list with the goal of nurturing leads, promoting products or services, delivering valuable content, or driving specific actions. We explore the various types of emails, such as newsletters, promotional emails, welcome sequences, and abandoned cart reminders. By leveraging email marketing, businesses can reach their audience directly, maintain regular communication, and foster customer loyalty.

Building a Quality Email List

A quality email list is essential for successful email marketing campaigns. We explore strategies for building an engaged and opt-in email subscriber base. Businesses should employ techniques such as offering lead magnets, creating compelling opt-in forms, utilizing social media promotions, and implementing customer segmentation.

By focusing on building a quality email list of interested and relevant subscribers, businesses can ensure higher open rates, click-through rates, and conversions.

Crafting Engaging Email Content

Engaging email content is crucial for capturing the attention and interest of subscribers. We discuss techniques for crafting compelling subject lines, writing personalized and relevant email copy, incorporating persuasive call-to-action buttons, and including visually appealing images or videos. Businesses should focus on delivering value, relevance, and a consistent brand voice in their email content. By providing valuable information, exclusive offers, or entertaining stories, businesses can keep subscribers engaged and encourage further interaction.

Email Automation and Segmentation

Automation takes email marketing to the next level by enabling businesses to deliver personalized, timely content to subscribers based on their behavior, preferences, or actions. We explore the power of email automation and segmentation in nurturing leads and driving conversions. Businesses can automate welcome emails, follow-up sequences, personalized recommendations, or re-engagement campaigns. By segmenting subscribers based on demographics, interests, or past interactions, businesses can deliver tailored content that resonates with individual subscribers, increasing engagement and conversion rates.

Optimizing Email Deliverability and Open Rates

Ensuring high email deliverability and open rates is essential for the success of email marketing campaigns. We discuss strategies for optimizing deliverability, including maintaining a clean and updated subscriber list, using double opt-in, avoiding spam trigger words, and adhering to email best practices. Additionally, we explore techniques for improving open rates, such as personalization, A/B testing subject lines, and optimizing preheader text. By following deliverability best practices and implementing strategies to increase open rates, businesses can maximize the effectiveness of their email marketing efforts.

Email Analytics and Performance Tracking

Measuring email marketing performance is crucial for evaluating the success of campaigns and making data-driven decisions. We discuss the importance of email analytics and tracking key metrics, such as open rates, click-through rates, conversion rates, and unsubscribe rates. By analyzing performance data, businesses can gain insights into subscriber behavior, identify areas for improvement, and optimize their email marketing strategies for better results. Continuous tracking and analysis enable businesses to refine their content, targeting, and automation to drive higher engagement and conversions.

By incorporating email marketing and automation into their strategies, businesses can effectively nurture leads, engage with customers, and drive conversions. Building a quality email list, crafting engaging content, leveraging automation and segmentation, optimizing deliverability and open rates, and tracking performance metrics all contribute to a successful email marketing strategy. Email marketing and automation provide businesses with a direct and personalized channel to connect with their audience, build brand loyalty, and achieve their marketing goals.

Designing Impactful Email Campaigns

In this chapter, we explore the strategies and best practices for designing impactful email campaigns that captivate recipients, drive engagement, and deliver desired results. A well-designed email campaign goes beyond content—it encompasses visual appeal, clear messaging, and effective calls-to-action. By implementing the following principles, businesses can create email campaigns that resonate with subscribers and achieve their marketing objectives.

Consistent Branding and Visual Identity

Consistency in branding is essential for creating a cohesive and memorable email campaign. Businesses should ensure that their email design reflects their brand identity, including color schemes, logo placement, and typography. Consistent branding builds brand recognition and reinforces the trust and familiarity subscribers have with the business.

Mobile-Friendly Design

Given the prevalence of mobile devices, designing emails that are mobile-friendly is crucial. Businesses should optimize their email layouts to be responsive and easily accessible on various screen sizes. This includes using a single-column layout, ensuring legibility of text and images, and optimizing button sizes for touch interactions. A seamless mobile experience ensures that subscribers can engage with the email content regardless of the device they use.

Compelling Subject Lines and Preheader Text

Subject lines and preheader text are the first elements subscribers see when they receive an email. Crafting compelling subject lines that grab attention and generate curiosity is essential to entice recipients to open the email. Additionally, optimizing preheader text—a brief summary or preview of the email content—can provide additional context and encourage opens. Clear and concise messaging in subject lines and preheader text sets the stage for the email's content.

Engaging and Relevant Content

The content within the email itself should be engaging, relevant, and tailored to the target audience. Businesses should focus on delivering valuable information, personalized recommendations, exclusive offers, or entertaining stories that resonate with subscribers. Utilizing dynamic content or personalization tokens based on subscriber data can further enhance the relevance and effectiveness of the email content.

Clear Calls-to-Action (CTAs)

Including clear and prominent calls-to-action (CTAs) is crucial for guiding recipients towards the desired action. CTAs should be visually distinct, compelling, and aligned with the email's objective. Businesses should use action-oriented language and position CTAs strategically within the email to maximize click-through rates. By providing a clear path for subscribers to take action, businesses can drive conversions and achieve their campaign goals.

Eye-Catching Visuals

Visual elements, such as images or videos, can significantly enhance the impact of an email campaign. Businesses should utilize eye-catching visuals that align with the email's purpose and support the message being conveyed. High-quality images, compelling graphics, or engaging videos can capture subscribers' attention and encourage them to continue reading or take action.

Testing and Optimization

Testing and optimizing email campaigns are essential for maximizing their impact. Businesses should conduct A/B tests on various elements, such as subject lines, CTAs, or email designs, to identify the most effective combinations. Additionally, analyzing performance metrics, such as open rates, click-through rates, and conversions, allows businesses to refine their campaigns and make data-driven improvements over time.

Personalization and Segmentation

Personalization and segmentation play a vital role in designing impactful email campaigns. By segmenting subscribers based on demographics, preferences, or past interactions, businesses can deliver highly targeted and personalized content. Tailoring the email messaging and offers to specific segments ensures relevance and increases the likelihood of engagement and conversions.

By implementing these design principles, businesses can create impactful email campaigns that stand out in subscribers' inboxes, drive engagement, and deliver the desired results. Consistent branding, mobile-friendly design, compelling subject lines and preheader text, engaging content, clear CTAs, eye-catching visuals, testing and optimization, and personalization and segmentation all contribute to the effectiveness of email campaigns and help businesses achieve their marketing objectives.

Implementing Marketing Automation Tools

In this chapter, we explore the implementation of marketing automation tools to streamline and enhance email marketing efforts. Marketing automation allows businesses to automate repetitive tasks, deliver personalized content, and nurture leads at scale. By leveraging marketing automation tools effectively, businesses can save time, improve efficiency, and deliver targeted messages that resonate with their audience.

Selecting the Right Marketing Automation Platform

The first step in implementing marketing automation is selecting the right platform that suits the business's needs. Businesses should evaluate different marketing automation tools based on features, scalability, ease of use, integration capabilities, and pricing. It's essential to choose a platform that aligns with the organization's goals and provides the necessary functionalities for email marketing automation, such as workflow automation, lead scoring, segmentation, and analytics.

Building Customer Journeys and Workflows

Marketing automation platforms enable businesses to build customer journeys and workflows that automate the delivery of emails based on predefined triggers, actions, or conditions. Businesses should map out the customer journey and identify touchpoints where automated emails can be sent to engage and nurture leads. Workflows can include welcome sequences, abandoned cart reminders, re-engagement campaigns, or personalized content based on subscriber behavior or interests.

Segmenting and Personalizing Email Campaigns

Segmentation and personalization are critical components of successful marketing automation. Businesses should utilize the segmentation capabilities of the automation platform to categorize subscribers based on demographics, behaviors, or interests. By segmenting the audience, businesses can send targeted and personalized emails that resonate with specific groups, increasing engagement and conversions. Personalization tokens can be used to dynamically insert subscriber-specific information into email content, creating a more tailored and relevant experience.

Lead Scoring and Nurturing

Marketing automation tools often include lead scoring functionalities that assign values to leads based on their engagement and interactions. By implementing lead scoring, businesses can identify and prioritize leads that are more likely to convert. Nurturing campaigns can be set up to automatically send targeted emails to leads at different stages of the sales funnel, providing them with relevant content and guiding them towards conversion.

Analyzing and Optimizing Campaign Performance

Marketing automation platforms provide robust analytics and reporting capabilities to track and measure the performance of email campaigns. Businesses should regularly analyze key metrics such as open rates, click-through rates, conversion rates, and revenue generated. By gaining insights into campaign performance, businesses can identify areas for improvement, make data-driven decisions, and optimize their email marketing strategies for better results.

Integrating with Other Marketing Channels

Marketing automation platforms often offer integration capabilities with other marketing channels and tools. Businesses should explore integration possibilities to enhance their overall marketing efforts. For example, integrating with customer relationship management (CRM) systems allows businesses to align sales and marketing activities seamlessly. Integrations with social media platforms or landing page builders can further expand the reach and impact of email marketing campaigns.

Continuous Learning and Improvement

Implementing marketing automation tools is an iterative process. Businesses should continuously learn from data, customer feedback, and market trends to improve their automation strategies. Regularly testing different approaches, analyzing results, and making adjustments based on insights contribute to ongoing optimization and success.

By effectively implementing marketing automation tools, businesses can automate email workflows, personalize content, nurture leads, and achieve greater efficiency in their email marketing efforts. Selecting the right platform, building customer journeys, segmenting and personalizing campaigns, lead scoring and nurturing, analyzing campaign performance, integrating with other channels, and embracing continuous improvement all play crucial roles in harnessing the power of marketing automation for email marketing success.

Designing Impactful Email Campaigns

In this chapter, we explore the strategies and best practices for designing impactful email campaigns that captivate recipients, drive engagement, and deliver desired results. A well-designed email campaign goes beyond content—it encompasses visual appeal, clear messaging, and effective calls-to-action. By implementing the following principles, businesses can create email campaigns that resonate with subscribers and achieve their marketing objectives.

Consistent Branding and Visual Identity

Consistency in branding is essential for creating a cohesive and memorable email campaign. Businesses should ensure that their email design reflects their brand identity, including color schemes, logo placement, and typography. Consistent branding builds brand recognition and reinforces the trust and familiarity subscribers have with the business.

Mobile-Friendly Design

Given the prevalence of mobile devices, designing emails that are mobile-friendly is crucial. Businesses should optimize their email layouts to be responsive and easily accessible on various screen sizes. This includes using a single-column layout, ensuring legibility of text and images, and optimizing button sizes for touch interactions. A seamless mobile experience ensures that subscribers can engage with the email content regardless of the device they use.

Compelling Subject Lines and Preheader Text

Subject lines and preheader text are the first elements subscribers see when they receive an email. Crafting compelling subject lines that grab attention and generate curiosity is essential to entice recipients to open the email. Additionally, optimizing preheader text—a brief summary or preview of the email content—can provide additional context and encourage opens. Clear and concise messaging in subject lines and preheader text sets the stage for the email's content.

Engaging and Relevant Content

The content within the email itself should be engaging, relevant, and tailored to the target audience. Businesses should focus on delivering valuable information, personalized recommendations, exclusive offers, or entertaining stories that resonate with subscribers. Utilizing dynamic content or personalization tokens based on subscriber data can further enhance the relevance and effectiveness of the email content.

Clear Calls-to-Action (CTAs)

Including clear and prominent calls-to-action (CTAs) is crucial for guiding recipients towards the desired action. CTAs should be visually distinct, compelling, and aligned with the email's objective. Businesses should use action-oriented language and position CTAs strategically within the email to maximize click-through rates. By providing a clear path for subscribers to take action, businesses can drive conversions and achieve their campaign goals.

Eye-Catching Visuals

Visual elements, such as images or videos, can significantly enhance the impact of an email campaign. Businesses should utilize eye-catching visuals that align with the email's purpose and support the message being conveyed. High-quality images, compelling graphics, or engaging videos can capture subscribers' attention and encourage them to continue reading or take action.

Testing and Optimization

Testing and optimizing email campaigns are essential for maximizing their impact. Businesses should conduct A/B tests on various elements, such as subject lines, CTAs, or email designs, to identify the most effective combinations. Additionally, analyzing performance metrics, such as open rates, click-through rates, and conversions, allows businesses to refine their campaigns and make data-driven improvements over time.

Personalization and Segmentation

Personalization and segmentation play a vital role in designing impactful email campaigns. By segmenting subscribers based on demographics, preferences, or past interactions, businesses can deliver highly targeted and personalized content. Tailoring the email messaging and offers to specific segments ensures relevance and increases the likelihood of engagement and conversions.

By implementing these design principles, businesses can create impactful email campaigns that stand out in subscribers' inboxes, drive engagement, and deliver the desired results. Consistent branding, mobile-friendly design, compelling subject lines and preheader text, engaging content, clear CTAs, eye-catching visuals, testing and optimization, and personalization and segmentation all contribute to the effectiveness of email campaigns and help businesses achieve their marketing objectives.

Implementing Marketing Automation Tools

In this chapter, we explore the implementation of marketing automation tools to streamline and enhance email marketing efforts. Marketing automation allows businesses to automate repetitive tasks, deliver personalized content, and nurture leads at scale. By leveraging marketing automation tools effectively, businesses can save time, improve efficiency, and deliver targeted messages that resonate with their audience.

Selecting the Right Marketing Automation Platform

The first step in implementing marketing automation is selecting the right platform that suits the business's needs. Businesses should evaluate different marketing automation tools based on features, scalability, ease of use, integration capabilities, and pricing. It's essential to choose a platform that aligns with the organization's goals and provides the necessary functionalities for email marketing automation, such as workflow automation, lead scoring, segmentation, and analytics.

Building Customer Journeys and Workflows

Marketing automation platforms enable businesses to build customer journeys and workflows that automate the delivery of emails based on predefined triggers, actions, or conditions. Businesses should map out the customer journey and identify touchpoints where automated emails can be sent to engage and nurture leads. Workflows can include welcome sequences, abandoned cart reminders, re-engagement campaigns, or personalized content based on subscriber behavior or interests.

Segmenting and Personalizing Email Campaigns

Segmentation and personalization are critical components of successful marketing automation. Businesses should utilize the segmentation capabilities of the automation platform to categorize subscribers based on demographics, behaviors, or interests. By segmenting the audience, businesses can send targeted and personalized emails that resonate with specific groups, increasing engagement and conversions. Personalization tokens can be used to dynamically insert subscriber-specific information into email content, creating a more tailored and relevant experience.

Lead Scoring and Nurturing

Marketing automation tools often include lead scoring functionalities that assign values to leads based on their engagement and interactions. By implementing lead scoring, businesses can identify and prioritize leads that are more likely to convert. Nurturing campaigns can be set up to automatically send targeted emails to leads at different stages of the sales funnel, providing them with relevant content and guiding them towards conversion.

Analyzing and Optimizing Campaign Performance

Marketing automation platforms provide robust analytics and reporting capabilities to track and measure the performance of email campaigns. Businesses should regularly analyze key metrics such as open rates, click-through rates, conversion rates, and revenue generated. By gaining insights into campaign performance, businesses can identify areas for improvement, make data-driven decisions, and optimize their email marketing strategies for better results.

Integrating with Other Marketing Channels

Marketing automation platforms often offer integration capabilities with other marketing channels and tools. Businesses should explore integration possibilities to enhance their overall marketing efforts. For example, integrating with customer relationship management (CRM) systems allows businesses to align sales and marketing activities seamlessly. Integrations with social media platforms or landing page builders can further expand the reach and impact of email marketing campaigns.

Continuous Learning and Improvement

Implementing marketing automation tools is an iterative process. Businesses should continuously learn from data, customer feedback, and market trends to improve their automation strategies. Regularly testing different approaches, analyzing results, and making adjustments based on insights contribute to ongoing optimization and success.

By effectively implementing marketing automation tools, businesses can automate email workflows, personalize content, nurture leads, and achieve greater efficiency in their email marketing efforts. Selecting the right platform, building customer journeys, segmenting and personalizing campaigns, lead scoring and nurturing, analyzing campaign performance, integrating with other channels, and embracing continuous improvement all play crucial roles in harnessing the power of marketing automation for email marketing success.

Personalization and Segmentation Strategies for Email Marketing

In this chapter, we delve into the importance of personalization and segmentation in email marketing and explore strategies to implement them effectively. Personalization and segmentation allow businesses to deliver targeted and relevant content to subscribers, resulting in higher engagement, increased conversions, and stronger customer relationships.

Understanding Personalization in Email Marketing

Personalization involves tailoring email content to individual subscribers based on their preferences, behavior, and demographics. It goes beyond simply addressing the recipient by their name—it encompasses customizing the email's content, offers, recommendations, and even the sending time. Personalization creates a more personalized and relevant experience for subscribers, making them feel valued and increasing their engagement with the email.

Importance of Segmentation in Email Marketing

Segmentation involves categorizing subscribers into distinct groups based on specific criteria, such as demographics, preferences, purchase history, or engagement level. By segmenting the audience, businesses can create targeted email campaigns that resonate with each group's unique characteristics and interests. Segmentation allows for more precise targeting, enabling businesses to deliver highly relevant content and offers, resulting in improved open rates, click-through rates, and conversions.

Collecting and Leveraging Subscriber Data

To personalize and segment effectively, businesses need to collect and leverage subscriber data. They can gather data through sign-up forms, preference centers, purchase history, website interactions, or surveys. This data provides valuable insights into subscribers' interests, preferences, and behaviors, enabling businesses to tailor their email campaigns accordingly. Leveraging subscriber data allows businesses to create highly targeted and personalized content that resonates with each individual.

Creating Dynamic Content

Dynamic content involves dynamically changing parts of an email based on the recipient's attributes or preferences. It allows businesses to customize email content based on subscriber data, delivering personalized recommendations, product suggestions, or location-specific offers. Dynamic content creates a more tailored experience for each subscriber, increasing their engagement and driving higher conversion rates.

Implementing Behavior-Based Triggers

Behavior-based triggers are automated emails triggered by specific subscriber actions or behaviors, such as making a purchase, abandoning a cart, or signing up for a newsletter. By setting up behavior-based triggers, businesses can send timely and relevant emails that respond to subscribers' actions. These triggered emails can include personalized product recommendations, reminders, or exclusive offers, providing a seamless and personalized customer experience.

Lifecycle Email Marketing

Lifecycle email marketing involves sending targeted emails at different stages of the customer lifecycle, from onboarding to retention and re-engagement. By understanding where subscribers are in their journey, businesses can send relevant emails that cater to their specific needs and interests. For example, new subscribers may receive a welcome series, while loyal customers may receive exclusive offers or loyalty rewards. Lifecycle email marketing nurtures customer relationships and encourages long-term engagement.

Testing and Optimizing Personalization and Segmentation

To ensure the effectiveness of personalization and segmentation strategies, businesses should continually test and optimize their email campaigns. A/B testing different personalization elements, segmenting criteria, or content variations helps identify the most effective approaches. Analyzing performance metrics, such as open rates, click-through rates, and conversions, provides insights into the effectiveness of personalization and segmentation efforts, allowing businesses to refine their strategies for better results.

By implementing personalization and segmentation strategies in email marketing, businesses can deliver targeted and relevant content that resonates with subscribers. Collecting and leveraging subscriber data, creating dynamic content, implementing behavior-based triggers, leveraging lifecycle email marketing, and continually testing and optimizing all contribute to successful personalization and segmentation. These strategies result in improved engagement, increased conversions, and stronger customer relationships, ultimately driving the success of email marketing campaigns.

Chapter 9
Influencer Marketing and Brand Partnerships

In this chapter, we explore the powerful strategy of influencer marketing and brand partnerships, which have become integral components of modern marketing campaigns. Influencer marketing leverages the reach and influence of individuals with significant online followings to promote products or services, while brand partnerships involve collaborating with other brands to create mutually beneficial marketing initiatives. By understanding and effectively implementing these strategies, businesses can expand their reach, enhance credibility, and drive meaningful engagement with their target audience.

Understanding Influencer Marketing

Influencer marketing involves collaborating with individuals who have established credibility and a loyal following in a specific niche or industry. Influencers, typically active on social media platforms such as Instagram, YouTube, or TikTok, have the power to sway the opinions and purchasing decisions of their followers. By partnering with influencers whose values align with their brand, businesses can tap into their reach, authenticity, and influence to promote their products or services to a highly engaged audience.

Identifying the Right Influencers

Choosing the right influencers is critical for the success of an influencer marketing campaign. Businesses should consider factors such as audience demographics, engagement rates, content quality, and brand alignment when selecting influencers. Micro-influencers, with smaller but highly engaged audiences, can be particularly effective for niche markets. Thorough research and analysis of influencers' content, audience demographics, and previous collaborations can help ensure a strong fit for the brand.

Developing Authentic Partnerships

Successful influencer marketing campaigns are built on authentic partnerships. It is essential for businesses to establish genuine relationships with influencers based on shared values and mutual respect. By involving influencers in the creative process and giving them the freedom to express their authentic opinions, businesses can ensure that the content resonates with both the influencer's audience and their brand message. Authenticity is key to building trust and credibility with the target audience.

Leveraging Different Types of Influencer Collaborations

Influencer marketing offers various collaboration options to suit different campaign goals and budgets. These include sponsored content, product placements, brand ambassadorships, or affiliate programs. Sponsored content involves influencers creating dedicated posts or videos promoting the brand or its products. Product placements feature the brand's products in influencers' content in a more organic manner. Brand ambassadorships involve longer-term partnerships with influencers representing the brand on an ongoing basis. Affiliate programs allow influencers to earn a commission for driving sales through their unique affiliate links. Choosing the right type of collaboration depends on the campaign objectives and target audience.

Harnessing the Power of Brand Partnerships

Brand partnerships involve collaborating with other complementary brands to create joint marketing initiatives. By aligning with like-minded brands, businesses can leverage each other's audience, expertise, and resources to amplify their marketing efforts and reach a broader consumer base. Brand partnerships offer opportunities for co-creating content, running joint promotions, hosting events, or developing co-branded products, benefiting both brands and providing unique value to the target audience.

Identifying Compatible Brand Partners

Finding compatible brand partners is crucial for successful collaborations. Businesses should seek brands that share similar values, target similar audiences, and complement their products or services. Collaborating with non-competitive brands allows for cross-promotion and access to a wider pool of potential customers. Thorough research and a shared vision for the partnership help ensure a strong fit and maximize the benefits for both brands involved.

Co-Creating Compelling Content

One of the key benefits of brand partnerships is the ability to co-create engaging content that resonates with both brands' audiences. By combining creative forces, brands can develop unique and compelling content that tells a cohesive story and provides value to the target audience. Co-created content can take various forms, including blog posts, videos, social media campaigns, or even joint events. The key is to ensure that the content aligns with the values and interests of both brands and delivers a seamless brand experience.

Amplifying Reach and Engagement

Brand partnerships offer the opportunity to tap into each other's existing audience and expand reach and engagement. By cross-promoting each other's products or services, both brands can expose their offerings to a new set of potential customers who may have a genuine interest in what they have to offer. Leveraging each other's social media channels, newsletters, or other marketing channels allows for wider exposure and increased engagement with the target audience.

Measuring and Evaluating Partnership Success

Measuring the success of brand partnerships is essential to gauge the effectiveness of the collaboration and make data-driven decisions for future initiatives. Businesses should establish clear objectives and key performance indicators (KPIs) at the outset of the partnership. Tracking metrics such as reach, engagement, website traffic, conversions, or customer acquisition can provide valuable insights into the impact of the partnership. Regular evaluation allows for ongoing optimization and the identification of successful partnership strategies.

By implementing influencer marketing and brand partnerships effectively, businesses can leverage the reach, credibility, and resources of influencers and complementary brands to enhance their marketing efforts. Identifying the right influencers, developing authentic partnerships, leveraging different collaboration types, identifying compatible brand partners, co-creating compelling content, amplifying reach and engagement, and measuring partnership success are all key elements of successful influencer marketing and brand partnership strategies.

Identifying relevant influencers for your brand is a crucial step in executing a successful influencer marketing campaign. The right influencers can help you reach your target audience, build brand awareness, and drive engagement and conversions. Here are some strategies to help you identify influencers that align with your brand:

Define your target audience

- Start by clearly defining your target audience and understanding their demographics, interests, and preferences. This will help you identify influencers whose followers match your ideal customer profile.

Conduct thorough research

Use social media platforms, influencer marketing platforms, and industry-related websites to research and identify influencers in your niche. Look for influencers who create content relevant to your industry and have a substantial and engaged following.

Analyze influencer metrics

Look beyond follower count and assess other key metrics to evaluate an influencer's relevance and impact. Consider factors such as engagement rate, reach, average likes and comments per post, and the quality of their content. Tools like social media analytics platforms or influencer marketing platforms can provide valuable insights.

Assess influencer authenticity and alignment

Authenticity is crucial in influencer marketing. Evaluate an influencer's content to ensure it aligns with your brand values, messaging, and aesthetics. Look for influencers who have a genuine connection with their audience and create content that resonates with their followers.

Consider influencer partnerships and collaborations

Look for influencers who have previously collaborated with brands in your industry or with similar target audiences. Assess the success and impact of these partnerships to gauge whether they would be a good fit for your brand.

Engage with influencers

Once you have identified potential influencers, engage with them on social media platforms. Interact with their content, leave meaningful comments, and start building a relationship. This can help you gauge their responsiveness and further assess their suitability for your brand.

Leverage influencer marketing platforms

Consider using influencer marketing platforms that connect brands with influencers. These platforms provide access to a vast network of influencers and offer advanced search and filtering options based on specific criteria, making it easier to find relevant influencers for your brand.

Consider micro-influencers

Don't overlook the potential of micro-influencers who have smaller but highly engaged followings. They often have a niche audience and can provide more targeted reach and higher engagement rates. Micro-influencers may also be more cost-effective for brands with limited budgets.

Remember, the key is to find influencers who authentically align with your brand and have an engaged audience that matches your target demographic. Building long-term relationships with influencers who genuinely support your brand can lead to fruitful and successful partnerships.

Negotiating partnerships and collaborations is a crucial step in establishing mutually beneficial relationships with other brands or influencers. Successful negotiations can lead to impactful marketing initiatives and open doors for new opportunities. Here are some strategies to help you navigate the negotiation process effectively:

Define your objectives

Clearly outline your objectives and what you aim to achieve through the partnership or collaboration. Identify the specific goals you want to accomplish, such as increasing brand awareness, reaching a new target audience, or driving sales. Having well-defined objectives will guide your negotiation strategy.

Research and gather information

Before entering into negotiations, gather information about the potential partner or influencer. Understand their values, target audience, past collaborations, and the value they can bring to your brand. This knowledge will help you tailor your negotiation approach and demonstrate your understanding of their unique value proposition.

Identify shared benefits

Highlight the benefits that both parties can gain from the partnership or collaboration. Consider what you can offer the other party in terms of exposure, access to your audience, or resources. Emphasize the synergies and opportunities for growth that arise from working together. Present a compelling case for why the collaboration is a win-win scenario.

Determine the scope and deliverables

Clearly define the scope of the partnership or collaboration, including the specific deliverables, timelines, and expectations from both parties. Discuss the types of content, campaigns, or activities you envision and ensure that both parties are aligned on the desired outcomes. This clarity will help avoid misunderstandings down the line.

Negotiate mutually beneficial terms

Negotiate terms that benefit both parties involved. This may include aspects such as compensation, revenue-sharing models, exclusivity, intellectual property rights, or promotional obligations. Find a balance that meets both parties' needs and aligns with the value each brings to the collaboration.

Maintain open and respectful communication

Throughout the negotiation process, maintain open and respectful communication with the potential partner or influencer. Listen to their perspectives, address any concerns, and be open to finding common ground. Effective communication builds trust and sets the foundation for a successful partnership.

Consider a trial period or pilot project

If you're unsure about committing to a long-term partnership, consider starting with a trial period or a pilot project. This allows you to test the collaboration on a smaller scale and assess its effectiveness before committing to a more extensive partnership. It also gives both parties an opportunity to evaluate the working dynamics and results.

Have a written agreement

Once negotiations are complete and terms are agreed upon, formalize the partnership or collaboration in a written agreement.

Include all agreed-upon terms, deliverables, timelines, and any other relevant details. Having a clear agreement protects both parties and ensures that expectations are met.

Remember that negotiations should be a collaborative process where both parties feel valued and benefit from the partnership. Be open to compromise, find creative solutions, and maintain a positive and professional approach throughout the negotiation process. Building strong partnerships and collaborations is a continuous process that requires ongoing communication, mutual respect, and a shared vision for success.

Measuring the effectiveness of influencer campaigns

Measuring the effectiveness of influencer campaigns is essential to evaluate their impact, optimize future strategies, and demonstrate return on investment. While each campaign may have unique objectives, there are several key metrics and strategies that can help you measure their effectiveness:

Reach and Impressions

Evaluate the reach and impressions generated by the influencer campaign. This includes measuring the total number of followers reached through the influencer's content and the number of times the content was viewed. These metrics provide insights into the campaign's overall exposure and potential audience reach.

Engagement Metrics

Assess the engagement generated by the influencer campaign, such as likes, comments, shares, and saves on social media platforms. Engagement metrics indicate how well the content resonated with the audience and the level of interaction it generated. Higher engagement rates typically indicate a more impactful campaign.

Click-through Rate (CTR)

Track the CTR to measure the effectiveness of driving traffic to your website or landing page. This metric indicates the percentage of users who clicked on the influencer's content and proceeded to visit your website. A higher CTR suggests that the campaign successfully drove traffic and piqued interest among the audience.

Conversions and Sales

Measure the number of conversions or sales directly attributed to the influencer campaign. This can be done by using unique tracking links, promo codes, or referral programs. Tracking conversions provides tangible evidence of the campaign's impact on driving actual business results.

Brand Mentions and Sentiment

Monitor brand mentions and sentiment associated with the influencer campaign. Analyze social media conversations, comments, and direct feedback to gauge the overall sentiment and perception of your brand among the audience. Positive brand mentions and sentiment indicate a successful influencer campaign that positively influenced brand perception.

Audience Growth

Assess any changes in your own social media following or email subscriber base during and after the influencer campaign. A surge in new followers or subscribers can indicate that the campaign successfully expanded your brand's audience and generated interest among new potential customers.

Surveys and Feedback

Gather direct feedback from your audience through surveys or polls to understand their perception, attitudes, and purchasing behavior resulting from the influencer campaign. This qualitative data provides valuable insights into the campaign's impact on brand perception, customer trust, and purchase intent.

Cost-Effectiveness

Evaluate the cost-effectiveness of the influencer campaign by comparing the incurred expenses with the achieved results. Calculate metrics such as cost per impression, cost per engagement, or cost per conversion to assess the efficiency of your investment in influencer marketing.

Long-Term Partnerships

Assess the potential for long-term partnerships with influencers based on their campaign performance. Consider metrics such as repeat collaborations, follower growth over time, and ongoing engagement to determine the influencer's long-term impact on your brand's growth and success.

Remember that measuring the effectiveness of influencer campaigns should align with your campaign objectives and be tailored to your specific goals. Use a combination of quantitative and qualitative metrics to gain a comprehensive understanding of the campaign's impact. Regularly review and analyze these metrics to refine your influencer strategies and improve future campaigns.

Chapter 10
Analytics and Performance Tracking

In today's digital marketing landscape, data-driven decision-making is crucial for optimizing campaigns and achieving optimal results. Chapter 10 delves into the importance of analytics and performance tracking, providing insights into how businesses can leverage data to measure the effectiveness of their marketing efforts and make informed decisions.

Understanding the Role of Analytics

Analytics involves the collection, analysis, and interpretation of data to gain insights into various aspects of marketing campaigns. It provides valuable information about audience behavior, campaign performance, and overall return on investment. By understanding the role of analytics, businesses can harness the power of data to optimize their strategies and drive better results.

Defining Key Performance Indicators (KPIs)

Defining key performance indicators (KPIs) is a crucial step in analytics and performance tracking. KPIs are measurable metrics that align with business objectives and indicate the success of marketing efforts. They can vary based on campaign goals and may include metrics such as conversion rates, click-through rates, customer acquisition costs, return on ad spend, or engagement rates. By setting clear KPIs, businesses can focus their efforts and track their progress effectively.

Implementing Web Analytics Tools

Web analytics tools, such as Google Analytics, provide businesses with valuable insights into website performance, user behavior, and conversion tracking. By implementing web analytics tools, businesses can track metrics like website traffic, bounce rates, session duration, and conversion funnels. These tools enable businesses to understand how visitors interact with their website, identify areas for improvement, and optimize user experience to drive better conversions.

Social Media Analytics

Social media platforms offer built-in analytics tools that provide insights into the performance of social media campaigns. These tools provide data on reach, engagement, follower growth, demographics, and content performance. By analyzing social media analytics, businesses can assess the effectiveness of their social media strategies, identify the types of content that resonate with their audience, and make data-driven decisions to enhance engagement and achieve their marketing goals.

Email Marketing Analytics

Email marketing platforms often offer robust analytics features that allow businesses to track email campaign performance. Metrics such as open rates, click-through rates, conversion rates, and unsubscribe rates provide insights into the effectiveness of email campaigns. By analyzing email marketing analytics, businesses can refine their email strategies, optimize content, and improve personalization to drive higher engagement and conversions.

Data-Driven Decision Making

Data-driven decision-making involves using insights derived from analytics to inform marketing strategies and tactics. By analyzing data and identifying patterns, businesses can make informed decisions that maximize their marketing ROI and drive better results.

Analyzing Campaign Performance

Analyzing campaign performance involves regularly assessing the performance of marketing campaigns against predefined KPIs. By reviewing data and analytics, businesses can identify which campaigns are successful, which strategies are driving the best results, and where improvements can be made. This analysis allows businesses to allocate resources effectively and optimize their marketing efforts.

A/B Testing and Optimization

A/B testing is a powerful technique that involves testing two or more variations of a marketing element to determine which performs better. By conducting A/B tests on variables such as ad creatives, landing page designs, email subject lines, or call-to-action buttons, businesses can identify the most effective elements and optimize their campaigns accordingly. A/B testing allows for data-driven decision-making and continuous improvement.

Customer Segmentation and Personalization

Analytics can help businesses understand their audience better through customer segmentation. By analyzing data on customer demographics, behaviors, and preferences, businesses can segment their audience into distinct groups. This segmentation enables personalized marketing strategies that resonate with specific customer segments, leading to higher engagement and conversions.

ROI Analysis

Measuring return on investment (ROI) is a critical aspect of data-driven decision-making. By analyzing data on campaign costs and the corresponding results, businesses can assess the effectiveness and profitability of their marketing efforts. ROI analysis helps identify which campaigns or channels deliver the highest returns, enabling businesses to allocate resources strategically and optimize their marketing spend.

Privacy and Data Security

In the era of data-driven marketing, businesses must prioritize privacy and data security. It is crucial to comply with relevant data protection regulations and ensure that customer data is collected, stored, and analyzed securely. By implementing robust data security measures and adhering to best practices, businesses can safeguard customer trust and maintain the integrity of their data-driven marketing practices.

By embracing analytics and performance tracking, businesses can gain valuable insights into their marketing campaigns, customer behavior, and overall performance. Through data-driven decision-making, businesses can optimize their strategies, enhance customer experiences, and achieve their marketing objectives more effectively. Analytics and performance tracking empower businesses to stay competitive in today's data-centric marketing landscape.

Setting up analytics tools (Google Analytics, etc.)

Setting up analytics tools, such as Google Analytics, is essential for businesses to gain valuable insights into website performance, user behavior, and conversion tracking. Here are the steps involved in setting up analytics tools:

Create an Account

Visit the website of the analytics tool you wish to use, such as Google Analytics (analytics.google.com), and create an account by providing the necessary information.

Set Up a Property

Once you have an account, set up a new property for your website within the analytics tool. Provide details such as the website URL, industry category, and time zone.

Obtain the Tracking Code

After setting up the property, the analytics tool will provide you with a tracking code snippet. This code needs to be added to every page of your website to collect data. Copy the tracking code provided by the analytics tool.

Add the Tracking Code to Your Website

Insert the tracking code into the HTML of your website. The code should be placed just before the closing </head> tag on every page of your website. This allows the analytics tool to collect data on user interactions and website performance.

Configure Goals and Conversion Tracking

Set up goals within the analytics tool to track specific actions on your website that indicate conversions, such as form submissions, purchases, or newsletter sign-ups. Configure conversion tracking to measure and attribute these actions to your marketing efforts accurately.

Enable E-commerce Tracking (If Applicable)

If your website includes an e-commerce platform, enable e-commerce tracking in the analytics tool. This feature allows you to track revenue, transactions, and other e-commerce-specific metrics to evaluate the performance of your online store.

Customize Reporting and Dashboards

Tailor the reporting and dashboard settings within the analytics tool to focus on the metrics that matter most to your business. Create custom reports, set up automated email reports, and build personalized dashboards to monitor the key performance indicators (KPIs) aligned with your marketing goals.

Link Other Platforms (If Applicable)

Integrate other platforms, such as advertising platforms or email marketing tools, with your analytics tool to gather comprehensive data and insights. This linking enables you to track and analyze the effectiveness of your marketing campaigns holistically.

Set Up Filters and Data Segmentation

Utilize filters and data segmentation features within the analytics tool to refine your data analysis. Filters can exclude internal traffic or include specific segments, while segmentation allows you to analyze data based on user demographics, behavior, or traffic sources.

Test and Verify Implementation

After setting up the analytics tool and adding the tracking code, verify that the implementation is working correctly. Visit your website and ensure that data is being captured in the analytics tool's reporting interface. Perform test conversions to confirm that goals and conversion tracking are functioning as expected.

Regularly Monitor and Analyze Data

Once the setup is complete, regularly monitor and analyze the data provided by the analytics tool. Evaluate key metrics, track trends, and gain insights into user behavior to make informed decisions and optimize your marketing strategies.

Setting up analytics tools like Google Analytics requires careful attention to detail and ongoing monitoring to ensure accurate data collection and analysis. By implementing these tools, businesses can gain valuable insights to improve website performance, optimize marketing efforts, and drive better results.

Analyzing key metrics and interpreting data

Analyzing key metrics and interpreting data is a crucial step in leveraging the insights provided by analytics tools. By understanding and interpreting the data, businesses can gain valuable insights into the performance of their marketing campaigns and make informed decisions to optimize their strategies. Here are the steps involved in analyzing key metrics and interpreting data effectively:

Identify Relevant Metrics

Begin by identifying the key metrics that align with your campaign objectives and business goals. These may include metrics such as website traffic, conversion rates, engagement rates, click-through rates, bounce rates, or revenue generated. Focus on the metrics that provide the most meaningful insights into your specific goals.

Set Benchmarks and Goals

Establish benchmarks and goals for each metric to provide context for your analysis. This allows you to compare current performance against past performance or industry standards. Clear benchmarks and goals enable you to evaluate the effectiveness of your marketing efforts and track progress over time.

Segment Data

Segmenting data allows you to analyze performance based on specific criteria such as demographics, traffic sources, or user behavior. By segmenting data, you can identify patterns, trends, and opportunities within different segments of your audience. This analysis helps tailor your marketing strategies to specific audience segments for improved targeting and engagement.

Conduct Comparative Analysis

Compare data across different time periods, campaigns, or segments to identify trends, patterns, and areas for improvement. Comparative analysis helps you understand the impact of specific marketing initiatives, identify successful strategies, and make data-driven decisions for future campaigns.

Look for Correlations and Causations

Identify correlations between different metrics and determine causations to understand how one metric may impact another. For example, analyze how changes in website traffic may influence conversion rates or how variations in ad spend affect revenue. Understanding these relationships can guide strategic decision-making and optimize campaign performance.

Use Visualization Techniques

Visualize data using charts, graphs, or dashboards to make it easier to interpret and identify trends. Visual representations of data can help identify patterns, outliers, and areas of focus more effectively than raw numbers. Visualization techniques facilitate data-driven storytelling and make it easier to communicate insights within your organization.

Seek Context and External Factors

Consider external factors that may have influenced the data, such as seasonality, market trends, or specific events. Understanding the external context helps provide a more comprehensive interpretation of the data and allows for more accurate decision-making.

Iterate and Optimize

Continuously analyze and interpret data to identify areas for optimization. Use the insights gained to refine your marketing strategies, test new approaches, and improve campaign performance. Regularly review and iterate your strategies based on data-driven insights to drive continuous improvement.

Apply Insights to Decision-Making

Finally, translate the insights gained from data analysis into actionable strategies and tactics. Use the insights to guide your marketing decisions, allocate resources effectively, and optimize your campaigns for better results.

By analyzing key metrics and interpreting data effectively, businesses can gain actionable insights to improve their marketing strategies and drive better results. Regular data analysis and interpretation help identify trends, uncover opportunities, and make data-driven decisions that lead to optimized campaigns and increased ROI.

Making data-driven decisions for continuous improvement

Making data-driven decisions for continuous improvement is a vital process in modern marketing. By leveraging data insights, businesses can optimize their strategies, enhance customer experiences, and achieve better results. Here are the steps involved in making data-driven decisions for continuous improvement:

Define Clear Objectives

Start by clearly defining your objectives and key performance indicators (KPIs) based on your business goals. These objectives should be specific, measurable, attainable, relevant, and time-bound (SMART). Clear objectives provide a framework for analyzing data and evaluating performance.

Collect Relevant Data

Gather relevant data from various sources, such as analytics tools, customer surveys, social media listening, and sales reports. Ensure that the data collected aligns with your defined objectives and helps answer specific questions about your marketing efforts.

Analyze and Interpret the Data

Analyze the collected data to identify patterns, trends, and insights. Use data visualization techniques, such as charts, graphs, and dashboards, to make it easier to interpret and communicate the findings. Look for correlations, causations, and anomalies within the data to gain a deeper understanding of the performance.

Compare Against Benchmarks

Compare your data against established benchmarks, industry standards, or past performance to assess progress and identify areas for improvement. Benchmarking helps provide context and highlights areas where your marketing efforts excel or fall short.

Identify Opportunities and Challenges

Use data insights to identify opportunities for optimization and areas where challenges exist. Identify strengths that can be capitalized on and weaknesses that need improvement. Determine where changes can be made to enhance performance and achieve better results.

Generate Hypotheses

Based on the data insights and identified opportunities, generate hypotheses or assumptions about potential actions or changes that could lead to improvement. These hypotheses should be based on data-driven insights and align with your objectives.

Test and Experiment

Design experiments or tests to validate the hypotheses and gather further data. This may involve A/B testing different marketing strategies, modifying website elements, or trying new advertising channels. Controlled experiments allow you to measure the impact of specific changes and assess their effectiveness.

Monitor and Measure Results

Continuously monitor and measure the results of your experiments or changes. Collect data on the performance of different variants or approaches to evaluate their impact on the defined KPIs. This ongoing measurement helps validate the effectiveness of your decisions and guides further adjustments.

Iterate and Optimize

Based on the results and insights gained, iterate and optimize your marketing strategies. Make data-driven decisions to refine your approaches, discard ineffective tactics, and prioritize high-performing initiatives. Continuously test, measure, and adjust to drive continuous improvement.

Communicate and Align

Communicate the insights and findings from data analysis to key stakeholders within your organization. Ensure that decision-makers and team members are aligned with the data-driven approach and understand the rationale behind strategic changes. Encourage a culture of data-driven decision-making throughout the organization.

By following these steps, businesses can harness the power of data to make informed decisions, optimize their marketing efforts, and drive continuous improvement. Embrace a cycle of data collection, analysis, experimentation, and optimization to achieve better results over time. Data-driven decision-making fosters a culture of agility, adaptability, and innovation, leading to enhanced marketing strategies and long-term success.

Chapter 11
Emerging Trends and Future of Digital Marketing

Chapter 11 explores the exciting world of emerging trends and the future of digital marketing. As technology continues to evolve and consumer behaviors shift, businesses must stay ahead of the curve to remain competitive and drive success in the digital landscape.

Artificial Intelligence (AI) and Machine Learning

Artificial Intelligence (AI) and Machine Learning are revolutionizing the digital marketing landscape. AI-powered tools and algorithms enable businesses to automate tasks, analyze vast amounts of data, and deliver personalized experiences to customers. From chatbots and virtual assistants to predictive analytics and recommendation engines, AI and Machine Learning are transforming how businesses engage with their audience and optimize marketing strategies.

Voice Search and Smart Speakers

The rise of voice search and smart speakers, such as Amazon Echo or Google Home, is changing the way consumers interact with technology. Voice-activated assistants have become an integral part of people's lives, and businesses must adapt their digital marketing strategies to accommodate this shift. Optimizing content for voice search, developing voice-based advertising, and creating seamless voice-enabled experiences are key considerations for the future of digital marketing.

Augmented Reality (AR) and Virtual Reality (VR)

Augmented Reality (AR) and Virtual Reality (VR) offer immersive experiences that bridge the gap between the digital and physical worlds. AR and VR technologies are increasingly being utilized in digital marketing to create interactive and engaging campaigns. From virtual product try-ons to immersive brand storytelling, AR and VR have the potential to captivate audiences and provide unique brand experiences.

Influencer Marketing Evolution

Influencer marketing continues to evolve as both businesses and consumers become more discerning. Authenticity, transparency, and long-term partnerships are becoming paramount in influencer collaborations. Micro-influencers, with their highly engaged niche audiences, are gaining prominence, and businesses are focusing on building meaningful relationships with influencers who align with their brand values. As influencer marketing matures, businesses need to adapt their strategies to ensure genuine connections and mutual value.

Personalization and Customer Experience

Personalization and customer experience will continue to be critical for digital marketing success. Customers expect tailored experiences that cater to their preferences and needs. Leveraging data insights, businesses can deliver personalized content, product recommendations, and targeted messaging. By understanding their audience and providing exceptional customer experiences across all touchpoints, businesses can foster loyalty, drive engagement, and gain a competitive edge.

Privacy and Data Protection

Privacy concerns and data protection regulations are reshaping the digital marketing landscape. Consumers are increasingly aware of their data rights and expect transparency and security from businesses. Stricter regulations, such as the General Data Protection Regulation (GDPR) and the California Consumer Privacy Act (CCPA), require businesses to handle personal data responsibly. Adhering to privacy guidelines and adopting transparent data practices will be crucial for maintaining consumer trust and compliance.

Mobile-First Approach and Progressive Web Apps

Mobile devices have become the primary gateway to the digital world, and a mobile-first approach is imperative for successful digital marketing. Optimizing websites and applications for mobile devices, creating seamless user experiences, and adopting Progressive Web App (PWA) technologies enable businesses to engage users effectively on their mobile devices. Mobile payments, location-based marketing, and mobile-centric advertising will continue to shape the future of digital marketing.

Data-driven Decision-making and Marketing Analytics

Data-driven decision-making and marketing analytics will remain at the core of digital marketing strategies. As the volume of data increases, businesses need to harness analytics tools and interpret data to gain actionable insights. Advanced analytics techniques, such as predictive analytics and customer journey mapping, will drive marketing strategies, optimize campaigns, and enhance customer experiences.

By embracing emerging trends and understanding the future of digital marketing, businesses can stay ahead of the curve and capitalize on new opportunities. Adapting to technological advancements, prioritizing personalization and customer experience, complying with privacy regulations, and leveraging data insights will be key to thriving in the ever-evolving digital landscape.

Exploring the latest trends and technologies

Exploring the latest trends and technologies is essential for businesses to stay competitive and leverage the full potential of digital marketing. In this rapidly evolving landscape, staying up to date with the latest trends and adopting emerging technologies can give businesses a significant advantage. Here are some of the latest trends and technologies shaping the digital marketing landscape:

Chatbots and Conversational Marketing

Chatbots powered by Artificial Intelligence (AI) are transforming customer interactions. They provide instant responses, personalized recommendations, and efficient customer support. Conversational marketing, through chatbots or messaging apps, enables businesses to engage with customers in real-time, deliver personalized experiences, and drive conversions.

Video Marketing and Live Streaming

Video content continues to dominate digital platforms, with the rise of platforms like YouTube, TikTok, and Instagram Reels. Businesses are utilizing video marketing to tell compelling stories, showcase products, and engage audiences. Live streaming has also gained popularity, allowing businesses to connect with their audience in real-time, host live events, and provide interactive experiences.

User-Generated Content (UGC)

User-generated content has become a powerful marketing tool. Encouraging customers to create and share content related to a brand or product builds authenticity, trust, and social proof. UGC campaigns, such as hashtags or contests, drive engagement, expand brand reach, and foster a sense of community.

Influencer Marketing Evolution

Influencer marketing continues to evolve, with a shift towards long-term partnerships and authentic brand collaborations. Micro-influencers, with their niche audiences and higher engagement rates, are gaining prominence. Brands are focusing on genuine connections, aligning with influencers who share their values, and co-creating meaningful content.

Personalization and Hyper-targeting

Customers expect personalized experiences, and hyper-targeting enables businesses to deliver relevant content to specific audiences. Utilizing data insights, businesses can segment their audience, deliver personalized recommendations, and tailor messaging based on individual preferences and behaviors.

Voice Search Optimization

The increasing prevalence of voice-activated assistants, such as Amazon Alexa and Google Assistant, has led to the growth of voice search. Optimizing content for voice search queries and understanding natural language processing is crucial for businesses to appear in voice search results and provide voice-friendly experiences.

Augmented Reality (AR) and Virtual Reality (VR)

AR and VR technologies are transforming digital experiences. Brands are utilizing AR for virtual try-ons, product visualizations, and immersive brand storytelling. VR is being employed for virtual tours, events, and interactive experiences. These technologies enhance engagement, provide unique brand experiences, and bridge the gap between the physical and digital worlds.

Social Commerce

Social media platforms are evolving into e-commerce hubs, allowing businesses to sell products directly within social media apps. Social commerce features, like shoppable posts and in-app checkout, streamline the purchase process, increase conversions, and provide a seamless shopping experience.

Data Privacy and Security

With increasing concerns about data privacy, businesses must prioritize the security and ethical use of customer data. Adhering to data protection regulations, obtaining consent, and implementing robust security measures are essential to maintain customer trust and comply with legal requirements.

Artificial Intelligence (AI) for Automation and Personalization

AI-powered tools and algorithms automate processes, analyze data, and enable personalization at scale. AI can automate email campaigns, personalize content recommendations, and optimize ad targeting, improving efficiency and delivering tailored experiences to customers.

Exploring these latest trends and technologies allows businesses to identify opportunities, engage customers effectively, and drive innovation in their digital marketing strategies. By embracing these trends and leveraging emerging technologies, businesses can stay ahead of the curve and thrive in the ever-evolving digital landscape.

Preparing for future shifts in the digital marketing landscape

Preparing for future shifts in the digital marketing landscape is crucial to ensure businesses remain agile, adaptable, and competitive. As technology advances, consumer behaviors change, and market dynamics evolve, it's essential to anticipate and proactively respond to these shifts. Here are some strategies for preparing for future shifts in the digital marketing landscape:

Stay Informed and Engage in Continuous Learning

Actively seek knowledge about emerging trends, technologies, and industry insights. Stay updated on the latest news, attend industry conferences, participate in webinars, and engage with thought leaders. Embrace a mindset of continuous learning to stay ahead of the curve and identify future shifts in the digital marketing landscape.

Foster an Innovative Culture

Encourage an environment that promotes innovation and experimentation within your organization. Foster a culture that embraces change, welcomes new ideas, and encourages team members to explore innovative strategies. Encourage collaboration across departments to generate fresh perspectives and drive innovation.

Embrace Data-Driven Decision-Making

Invest in robust analytics tools, develop data-driven capabilities, and establish processes for collecting, analyzing, and interpreting data. Leverage data insights to make informed decisions, identify trends, and uncover opportunities. Adopt a culture of data-driven decision-making to optimize marketing strategies and drive better results.

Emphasize Customer-Centricity

Put the customer at the center of your digital marketing efforts. Invest in understanding customer needs, preferences, and behaviors through market research, surveys, and customer feedback. Anticipate customer expectations and align your strategies to deliver exceptional customer experiences across all touchpoints.

Develop an Agile Marketing Approach

Adopt an agile marketing approach that allows you to respond quickly to market shifts and adapt your strategies accordingly. Embrace iterative planning, frequent testing, and the ability to pivot based on data and customer feedback. Emphasize flexibility and nimbleness in your marketing operations.

Leverage Automation and Artificial Intelligence (AI)

Explore the potential of automation and AI technologies to streamline marketing processes, enhance efficiency, and deliver personalized experiences at scale. Automate repetitive tasks, leverage AI algorithms for data analysis, and deploy AI-powered chatbots for customer interactions. Stay informed about emerging automation and AI solutions that can benefit your marketing efforts.

Build Strong Partnerships

Foster strategic partnerships with technology providers, agencies, and industry experts who can help you navigate future shifts in the digital marketing landscape. Collaborate with partners who bring specialized expertise and innovative solutions to stay at the forefront of emerging trends and technologies.

Anticipate Regulatory Changes

Stay informed about evolving data privacy regulations and ensure compliance with relevant laws. Anticipate potential changes in data protection and privacy regulations that may impact your marketing strategies. Adopt transparent data practices and prioritize consumer privacy to maintain trust and build long-term relationships with customers.

Monitor Competitors and Industry Trends

Keep a close eye on your competitors' activities and industry trends. Monitor their digital marketing strategies, new initiatives, and customer engagement approaches. Learn from their successes and failures, adapt strategies based on market dynamics, and differentiate your brand to stay ahead of the competition.

Foster an Agile Digital Infrastructure

Ensure your digital infrastructure is scalable, adaptable, and capable of accommodating future technological advancements. Invest in robust content management systems, scalable hosting solutions, and flexible technology frameworks that can support the integration of new tools and platforms.

By preparing for future shifts in the digital marketing landscape, businesses can position themselves for success in an ever-changing environment. By staying informed, embracing innovation, leveraging data, and focusing on customer-centricity, businesses can proactively adapt to emerging trends and technologies, enabling them to thrive in the digital marketplace.

Harnessing the power of artificial intelligence and automation

Harnessing the power of artificial intelligence (AI) and automation has become increasingly important in the digital marketing landscape. AI and automation technologies offer businesses the ability to streamline processes, optimize campaigns, and deliver personalized experiences at scale. Here's how businesses can leverage AI and automation in their digital marketing strategies:

Data Analysis and Insights

AI-powered tools can analyze vast amounts of data and extract valuable insights. Machine learning algorithms can identify patterns, trends, and correlations within data sets, enabling businesses to make data-driven decisions. By leveraging AI for data analysis, businesses can uncover actionable insights that drive marketing strategies and optimize campaign performance.

Personalization at Scale

AI and automation enable businesses to deliver personalized experiences to customers at scale. By leveraging customer data, AI algorithms can segment audiences, create customer profiles, and deliver targeted messaging and recommendations. Personalization enhances customer engagement, increases conversions, and fosters long-term loyalty.

Chatbots and Virtual Assistants

Chatbots and virtual assistants powered by AI enhance customer interactions and provide real-time support. These intelligent chat systems can handle customer queries, assist with product recommendations, and provide personalized assistance. Chatbots help businesses provide instant responses, improve customer satisfaction, and free up human resources for more complex tasks.

Marketing Automation

Marketing automation platforms enable businesses to automate repetitive marketing tasks and workflows. From email campaigns to social media scheduling, automation streamlines processes, saves time, and ensures consistent messaging across channels. Businesses can create personalized customer journeys, nurture leads, and trigger relevant communications based on user behavior.

Predictive Analytics

AI-driven predictive analytics helps businesses anticipate customer behavior, trends, and outcomes. By analyzing historical data, predictive models can forecast future customer preferences, identify high-value leads, and optimize marketing strategies. Predictive analytics empowers businesses to make proactive decisions and take strategic actions for better results.

Content Creation and Curation

AI technology can assist in content creation and curation. Natural Language Processing (NLP) algorithms can generate written content, automate social media posts, and personalize content recommendations based on user preferences. AI tools can also curate relevant content from various sources, saving time and effort in content discovery.

Ad Optimization

AI-powered algorithms can optimize digital advertising campaigns in real-time. These algorithms analyze user behavior, campaign performance, and market trends to adjust bidding strategies, target specific audience segments, and allocate ad spend more effectively. AI-driven ad optimization maximizes ROI and improves ad targeting accuracy.

Voice Search and SEO

AI technologies play a significant role in voice search optimization. Natural Language Processing allows search engines to understand spoken queries better, and businesses can leverage AI to optimize their website content for voice search. By integrating voice search strategies into their SEO efforts, businesses can capture voice-based search traffic and enhance their visibility.

Social Media Management

AI tools assist in social media management by analyzing content performance, suggesting optimal posting times, and automating social media responses. AI algorithms can also identify trending topics, sentiment analysis, and competitor analysis, providing insights to optimize social media strategies.

Customer Insights and Sentiment Analysis

AI-powered sentiment analysis tools help businesses monitor social media conversations, customer reviews, and online mentions. By analyzing sentiment, businesses gain insights into customer perception, feedback, and brand reputation. AI tools enable businesses to identify emerging trends, address customer concerns promptly, and proactively engage with their audience.

By harnessing the power of AI and automation, businesses can streamline processes, gain valuable insights, enhance personalization, and optimize their digital marketing strategies. Embracing these technologies empowers businesses to deliver exceptional customer experiences, drive better results, and stay competitive in the ever-evolving digital landscape.

Chapter 12
Creating an Actionable Digital Marketing Plan

Chapter 12 focuses on creating an actionable digital marketing plan that aligns with business objectives and enables businesses to achieve their marketing goals effectively. A well-structured and comprehensive digital marketing plan provides a roadmap for implementing strategies, allocating resources, and measuring success. Here's how businesses can create an actionable digital marketing plan:

Define Objectives and Key Results (OKRs)

Start by clearly defining your marketing objectives and key results. These objectives should be specific, measurable, attainable, relevant, and time-bound (SMART). Align your objectives with your overall business goals to ensure that your digital marketing efforts contribute to the broader organizational strategy. Establish key metrics to track progress and measure success.

Conduct Market Research and Customer Analysis

Conduct thorough market research to understand your target market, industry trends, and competitive landscape. Analyze customer behavior, preferences, and pain points to tailor your marketing strategies accordingly. Identify market opportunities, emerging trends, and potential challenges that may impact your digital marketing plan. A deep understanding of your target audience will inform your messaging, channels, and tactics.

Develop Targeted Buyer Personas

Create detailed buyer personas that represent your ideal customers. These personas are fictional representations of your target audience, including demographic information, motivations, challenges, and preferred communication channels. Developing buyer personas helps you understand your customers' needs, customize your marketing messages, and engage with them more effectively.

Determine Digital Marketing Channels and Tactics

Based on your market research and buyer personas, identify the digital marketing channels and tactics that are most relevant to your target audience. Consider channels such as search engine marketing, social media marketing, email marketing, content marketing, and influencer partnerships. Select the channels and tactics that align with your objectives, resonate with your audience, and provide the best opportunities for reaching and engaging your target market.

Set Budget and Allocate Resources

Determine your digital marketing budget and allocate resources accordingly. Consider the costs associated with different channels, tools, advertising campaigns, content creation, and personnel. Allocate resources based on the channels and tactics that are most effective in reaching your target audience and driving desired outcomes. Continually monitor and adjust your budget allocation as needed based on performance and return on investment (ROI).

Develop Content Strategy and Editorial Calendar

Create a content strategy that aligns with your objectives, target audience, and digital channels. Determine the types of content that will resonate with your audience, such as blog posts, videos, infographics, or podcasts. Develop an editorial calendar that outlines content creation, publication dates, and distribution across various channels. Ensure your content is valuable, engaging, and optimized for search engines to drive organic traffic and audience engagement.

Implement Conversion Optimization Strategies

Focus on optimizing your digital assets and conversion funnels to maximize conversions. Implement strategies such as A/B testing, website optimization, landing page optimization, and call-to-action optimization. Continuously analyze and refine your conversion process to improve user experience, reduce friction, and increase conversion rates.

Establish Key Performance Indicators (KPIs) and Measurement Plan

Define key performance indicators (KPIs) that align with your objectives and track the success of your digital marketing efforts. Metrics may include website traffic, conversion rates, engagement metrics, customer acquisition costs, or return on ad spend. Develop a measurement plan that outlines how you will collect, analyze, and report on these metrics. Utilize analytics tools and reporting dashboards to monitor and track your performance regularly.

Regularly Evaluate and Adjust

Regularly evaluate the performance of your digital marketing efforts against your defined KPIs. Analyze data, review insights, and measure outcomes to identify areas of success and areas for improvement. Continually adapt and adjust your strategies based on data-driven insights, market shifts, and customer feedback. Embrace an iterative approach, testing new tactics, and optimizing your campaigns to drive continuous improvement.

Monitor Industry Trends and Emerging Technologies

Stay abreast of industry trends, emerging technologies, and shifts in consumer behavior. Continuously monitor changes in digital marketing platforms, algorithms, regulations, and customer preferences. Incorporate new trends and technologies that align with your objectives and have the potential to enhance your digital marketing efforts.

By following these steps and creating an actionable digital marketing plan, businesses can strategically execute their marketing initiatives, allocate resources effectively, and measure the success of their efforts. A well-designed plan provides guidance and direction, ensuring that businesses are equipped to navigate the dynamic digital marketing landscape and achieve their marketing goals.

Pulling all the elements together into a cohesive plan

Pulling all the elements together into a cohesive plan is the final step in creating a comprehensive and actionable digital marketing strategy. This process involves integrating the various components, aligning them with business goals, and creating a roadmap for implementation. Here's how businesses can pull all the elements together into a cohesive plan:

Start with a Clear Executive Summary

Summarize the key components of the digital marketing plan in an executive summary. Provide an overview of the objectives, target audience, selected channels, and expected outcomes. This summary should concisely communicate the essence of the plan to stakeholders and decision-makers.

Outline the Strategy

Present a detailed outline of the digital marketing strategy. Include sections on market research, buyer personas, selected channels and tactics, content strategy, conversion optimization, and measurement plan. Each section should provide clear objectives, actionable steps, and expected outcomes.

Define Roles and Responsibilities

Clearly define the roles and responsibilities of team members involved in executing the digital marketing plan. Assign tasks and establish accountability to ensure effective implementation. Outline the necessary resources, including budget allocation and technology requirements.

Establish a Timeline

Develop a timeline that outlines the key milestones, deliverables, and deadlines for each phase of the digital marketing plan. This timeline ensures that the plan is executed in a timely manner and allows for tracking progress throughout the implementation process.

Integrate with Overall Marketing Plan

Align the digital marketing plan with the broader marketing strategy and overall business goals. Ensure that the digital marketing efforts complement and support other marketing initiatives. This integration fosters consistency in messaging, maximizes impact, and enhances the overall effectiveness of marketing efforts.

Monitor and Evaluate

Establish a system for ongoing monitoring and evaluation of the digital marketing plan. Regularly review key performance indicators

(KPIs) and assess the effectiveness of different tactics and channels. Identify areas of success and areas that require adjustment or optimization. Make data-driven decisions to refine the plan and drive continuous improvement.

Communicate and Collaborate

Foster open communication and collaboration among team members involved in executing the digital marketing plan. Regularly share progress updates, insights, and results. Encourage feedback, brainstorming sessions, and knowledge sharing to leverage the collective expertise of the team.

Stay Agile and Adapt

Recognize that the digital marketing landscape is dynamic and subject to change. Stay informed about emerging trends, technologies, and shifts in consumer behavior. Embrace an agile mindset, allowing for flexibility and adaptation as needed. Continuously refine and optimize the plan to capitalize on new opportunities and address evolving challenges.

By pulling all the elements together into a cohesive plan, businesses can effectively execute their digital marketing strategies, align them with business goals, and drive success in the ever-evolving digital landscape. The cohesive plan provides a roadmap for implementation, facilitates communication and collaboration, and enables ongoing monitoring and optimization to achieve desired outcomes.

Budgeting and resource allocation

Budgeting and resource allocation are critical components of a successful digital marketing plan. Proper allocation of resources ensures that marketing initiatives are executed effectively and aligns with the overall business strategy. Here's how businesses can approach budgeting and resource allocation for their digital marketing efforts:

Define Budget Objectives

Start by defining clear budget objectives that align with your overall business goals. Consider the desired outcomes of your digital marketing plan, such as increasing brand awareness, driving website traffic, generating leads, or boosting sales. These objectives will guide your budget allocation decisions.

Assess Available Resources

Evaluate the resources available for digital marketing, including personnel, technology, and financial resources. Take into account the expertise and skills of your team members, existing marketing tools and platforms, and the financial capacity of your business. Assessing available resources helps determine the scope and scale of your digital marketing initiatives.

Prioritize Marketing Channels and Tactics

Based on your target audience, market research, and business objectives, prioritize the digital marketing channels and tactics that will yield the best results. Allocate a portion of your budget to each selected channel or tactic, considering their potential reach, effectiveness, and cost.

Consider Fixed and Variable Costs

Differentiate between fixed and variable costs in your digital marketing budget. Fixed costs are ongoing expenses, such as software subscriptions or salaries, while variable costs depend on campaign-specific needs, such as advertising spend or content creation costs.

Allocating resources to fixed and variable costs will help manage and track expenses more effectively.

Test and Optimize

Consider allocating a portion of your budget for testing and experimentation. This allows you to try new strategies, channels, or tactics on a smaller scale and evaluate their effectiveness before scaling up. Testing helps optimize your budget allocation by focusing resources on the most impactful approaches.

Account for Campaign Lifecycles

Consider the lifecycle of your digital marketing campaigns when allocating resources. Some campaigns may require more resources during the initial launch phase, while others may require ongoing maintenance and optimization. Allocate resources accordingly to ensure continuous support throughout the campaign lifecycle.

Monitor and Adjust

Regularly monitor the performance of your digital marketing initiatives and track the return on investment (ROI) of each channel and tactic. Use analytics and reporting tools to measure key performance indicators (KPIs) and assess the effectiveness of your budget allocation. Based on the insights gained, adjust your resource allocation to optimize your marketing efforts.

Explore Partnerships and Outsourcing

Consider partnering with external agencies, freelancers, or consultants to leverage specialized expertise and optimize resource allocation. Outsourcing certain tasks or projects can provide cost savings and access to a wider range of skills and capabilities, allowing your team to focus on core competencies.

Keep Pace with Industry Trends

Stay informed about evolving industry trends, emerging technologies, and changes in digital marketing platforms. Allocate resources to research and training to ensure your team remains up to date with the latest developments. Investing in learning and development ensures that your resources are well-equipped to execute effective digital marketing strategies.

Continuously Evaluate ROI

Regularly evaluate the return on investment of your digital marketing initiatives. Assess the impact of your allocated resources on the achievement of your marketing objectives. By analyzing ROI, you can make data-driven decisions to optimize your budget allocation and allocate resources to the channels and tactics that provide the highest ROI.

Effective budgeting and resource allocation are essential for maximizing the impact of your digital marketing efforts. By aligning resources with objectives, monitoring performance, and making data-driven adjustments, businesses can optimize their budget allocation, drive better results, and achieve their marketing goals efficiently.

Monitoring, testing, and optimizing strategies

Monitoring, testing, and optimizing strategies are vital components of a successful digital marketing plan. By continuously assessing the performance of your marketing initiatives, testing new approaches, and optimizing your strategies, you can improve outcomes and maximize return on investment. Here's how businesses can approach monitoring, testing, and optimizing their digital marketing strategies:

Establish Key Performance Indicators (KPIs)

Define clear and measurable KPIs that align with your objectives. These KPIs could include website traffic, conversion rates, engagement metrics, customer acquisition costs, or revenue generated. Establishing KPIs provides a benchmark for evaluating the success of your strategies and identifying areas for improvement.

Utilize Analytics Tools

Implement robust analytics tools, such as Google Analytics, to track and analyze the performance of your digital marketing efforts. These tools provide valuable insights into user behavior, traffic sources, conversion funnels, and campaign performance. Regularly review your analytics data to understand trends, identify strengths and weaknesses, and make data-driven decisions.

Conduct A/B Testing

A/B testing, also known as split testing, involves comparing two versions of a webpage, advertisement, or email to determine which performs better. Test different elements, such as headlines, calls-to-action, visuals, or landing page layouts. Analyze the results to identify winning variations and optimize your marketing assets based on user preferences.

Monitor Conversion Funnel Performance

Evaluate the effectiveness of your conversion funnels by tracking user journeys and identifying areas of drop-off or friction. Use analytics data to pinpoint where users abandon the funnel and implement optimizations to improve conversion rates. Streamline the user experience, simplify forms, and provide clear calls-to-action to enhance conversion rates.

Gather and Act on Customer Feedback

Actively seek customer feedback through surveys, social media listening, or customer support interactions. Pay attention to customer preferences, pain points, and suggestions for improvement. Leverage this feedback to refine your strategies, address customer concerns, and enhance the overall customer experience.

Keep Pace with Industry Trends

Stay informed about the latest industry trends, emerging technologies, and shifts in consumer behavior. Regularly assess how these trends may impact your target audience and marketing strategies. Experiment with new channels, tactics, or technologies that align with your objectives and have the potential to drive better results.

Optimize Content for Search Engines

Continuously optimize your website content for search engines to improve organic visibility and drive traffic. Conduct keyword research, optimize meta tags, improve website load times, and enhance mobile-friendliness. Monitor search engine rankings and adjust your optimization strategies to stay competitive and improve your visibility.

Leverage Retargeting and Remarketing

Implement retargeting and remarketing campaigns to re-engage users who have shown interest in your products or services. Target users who have visited your website, abandoned their carts, or interacted with specific content. Use tailored messaging and offers to encourage conversions and boost customer retention.

Embrace Agile Marketing Practices

Adopt an agile marketing approach that allows for flexibility and quick adjustments. Continually evaluate the performance of your campaigns, adapt your strategies based on data insights, and prioritize initiatives that deliver the best results. Agile practices empower you to respond to market changes, customer feedback, and emerging opportunities swiftly.

Continuous Learning and Improvement

Foster a culture of continuous learning and improvement within your marketing team. Encourage knowledge sharing, attend industry events, participate in webinars, and stay updated with the latest digital marketing practices. Invest in training and professional development to ensure your team remains skilled and adaptable in an ever-changing landscape.

By monitoring, testing, and optimizing your digital marketing strategies, you can identify areas for improvement, enhance customer experiences, and drive better results. The iterative process of testing and optimization allows you to refine your approaches, uncover new opportunities, and stay ahead of the competition in the dynamic digital marketing landscape.

In conclusion, a well-crafted and comprehensive digital marketing strategy is crucial for businesses to thrive in today's competitive landscape. By harnessing the power of digital marketing, businesses can effectively reach and engage their target audience, drive brand awareness, and achieve their marketing objectives. Throughout this book, we have explored various aspects of digital marketing, starting from understanding the digital marketing landscape and its evolution to the importance of setting goals, building effective strategies, and leveraging key digital marketing channels.

- We delved into the significance of website optimization, user experience, content marketing, social media marketing, search engine marketing, email marketing, influencer partnerships, analytics, and emerging trends shaping the future of digital marketing. Each chapter provided valuable insights, practical tips, and actionable strategies to help businesses navigate the digital landscape and drive growth.

- We emphasized the importance of staying informed about industry trends, leveraging the power of artificial intelligence and automation, and continuously monitoring, testing, and optimizing digital marketing strategies. By aligning these elements into a cohesive digital marketing plan, businesses can effectively allocate resources, track performance, adapt to changes, and achieve desired outcomes.

- The digital marketing landscape is ever-evolving, presenting both opportunities and challenges. It requires businesses to stay agile, embrace innovation, and adopt a customer-centric approach. By constantly analyzing data, monitoring consumer behavior, and leveraging emerging technologies, businesses can stay ahead of the curve and deliver exceptional experiences to their target audience.

- Ultimately, success in digital marketing lies in a combination of creativity, strategic thinking, data-driven decision-making, and adaptability. By implementing the principles and strategies outlined in this book, businesses can position themselves for success, connect with their customers in meaningful ways, and achieve sustainable growth in the digital era.

- As the digital marketing landscape continues to evolve, it is crucial for businesses to stay informed, adapt to changes, and embrace emerging technologies and trends. By doing so, businesses can position themselves for success and drive impactful results in the ever-changing digital landscape.

Conclusion

In the final chapter, we bring together the main findings and insights from each chapter, underscoring the significance of ongoing learning and flexibility in the ever-evolving realm of digital marketing. Throughout this book, we have explored various facets of digital marketing and demonstrated its immense capacity to revolutionize businesses, propel growth, and facilitate long-term triumph. By adopting the knowledge and suggestions presented in these pages, readers will gain the necessary tools to navigate the intricate intricacies of the digital marketing arena and harness its potential for their own benefit.

One of the fundamental messages conveyed throughout this book is the importance of adaptability in the face of rapid technological advancements and shifting consumer behaviors. The digital landscape is characterized by constant change, and successful marketers must be willing to embrace innovation and continuously refine their strategies. This book has served as a guide to understanding the dynamics of this ever-changing environment, equipping readers with the insights needed to adapt their marketing approaches and stay ahead of the competition.

Furthermore, we have explored a multitude of digital marketing techniques and tactics, shedding light on their transformative power when implemented effectively. From search engine optimization (SEO) to social media marketing, from content creation to data analytics, each chapter has delved into the intricacies of these strategies, providing practical advice and real-world examples to illustrate their potential impact. Armed with this knowledge, readers will be able to leverage these tools to build brand awareness, engage with their target audience, and drive meaningful business outcomes.

In addition, this book has emphasized the crucial role of data-driven decision-making in digital marketing. In today's digital age, vast amounts of data are generated every second, offering valuable insights into customer preferences, behaviors, and trends. We have explored the significance of collecting, analyzing, and interpreting data to inform marketing strategies, enabling marketers to make informed decisions and optimize their campaigns for maximum effectiveness. By embracing data-driven approaches, businesses can enhance their understanding of their target audience, refine their messaging, and allocate resources more efficiently.

Moreover, we have addressed the increasing importance of personalization in digital marketing. With consumers being inundated with a multitude of marketing messages every day, tailoring content and experiences to individual preferences has become paramount. We have discussed the power of segmentation, targeting, and personalized messaging, showcasing how these strategies can foster stronger connections with customers and drive higher levels of engagement. By understanding their audience and delivering relevant, personalized experiences, marketers can create meaningful relationships and cultivate brand loyalty.

Throughout this book, we have also explored the ethical dimensions of digital marketing. As technology advances, marketers must be cognizant of the ethical considerations surrounding data privacy, transparency, and consumer trust. We have emphasized the significance of adopting ethical practices and ensuring the responsible use of customer data. By prioritizing ethical considerations, businesses can build trust, enhance their reputation, and establish long-lasting relationships with their audience.

In conclusion, this book has provided a comprehensive overview of the dynamic field of digital marketing. By summarizing the key takeaways from each chapter, we have highlighted the transformative potential of digital marketing strategies and techniques. From adaptability to data-driven decision-making, personalization to ethical considerations, each aspect has been explored to equip readers with the knowledge and tools they need to thrive in the digital marketing landscape. As technology continues to evolve and consumer behaviors evolve along with it, continuous learning and adaptation will be vital for sustained success. By implementing the insights and recommendations presented in this book, readers will be well-positioned to navigate the complexities of digital marketing, stay ahead of the curve, and leverage the vast opportunities it offers to drive business growth and achieve long-term success.

www.ingramcontent.com/pod-product-compliance
Lightning Source LLC
LaVergne TN
LVHW061549070526
838199LV00077B/6965